STRANGE AND
MYSTERIOUS
STUFF FROM THE
BIBLE

STRANGE AND MYSTERIOUS STUFF FROM THE BIBLE

STEPHEN M. MILLER

HARVEST HOUSE PUBLISHERS
EUGENE, OREGON

Cover design by Knail, Salem, Oregon

Cover photos © Don Farrall/Photodisc/Getty Images

Published in association with the literary agency of The Steve Laube Agency, LLC, 5025 N. Central Ave., #635, Phoenix, Arizona, 85012.

STRANGE AND MYSTERIOUS STUFF FROM THE BIBLE
Copyright © 2014 by Stephen M. Miller
Published by Harvest House Publishers
Eugene, Oregon 97402
www.harvesthousepublishers.com

Library of Congress Cataloging-in-Publication Data
   Miller, Stephen M.
   Strange and mysterious stuff from the Bible / Stephen M. Miller.
      pages cm
   ISBN 978-0-7369-5698-7 (pbk.)
   ISBN 978-0-7369-5699-4 (eBook)
   1. Bible—Miscellanea. I. Title.
   BS615.M56 2014
   220.6—dc23

                                                2013043564

Printed in the United States of America

14 15 16 17 18 19 20 21 22 / VP-CD / 10 9 8 7 6 5 4 3 2 1

CONTENTS

INTRODUCTION

Reading the Bible, as far as I'm concerned, is a bit like riding in the car to Grandpap's house when I was a kid.

Grandpap and Granny lived in a holler about two miles off the paved road outside Tunnelton, West Virginia. That last stretch of road—if you could call it a road—served up one doozy of a ride. Coal trucks and Mother Nature left their mark on this dirt trail that someone sprinkled with gravel.

Dad tried to dodge the biggest potholes so the car wouldn't bottom out, but he couldn't miss them all. On some stretches, it felt like he hit them all.

I'd usually ride shotgun because I was the oldest of five kids. Mom generally sat in the back, tending the youngest three. We'd be riding along on that coal truck trail, and suddenly the front of the car would take an elevator dip to the right or left—as though we were about to drive off the corner of the planet.

Bumpy Bible Road

I hit bumps in the road when I read the Bible. We all do. We're cruising along reading a fine little story when all of a sudden, we hit a jaw-dropper of a narrative pothole. Right out loud we might say, "In heaven's name, what on earth is this doing in God's holy Word?" For example…

- Jewish law requires a rapist to marry his virgin victim (see item number 1).

- God kills 70,000 Jews with a plague because of one man's sin (see number 20).

- Good people die young because God is protecting them from evil (see number 15).

Well, kick me in the gut and call me a comma. It's time for a pause.

This is a Bible bump book. A travelogue of sorts. It's my best effort to prepare you for the road ahead, which is going to jar you from time to time. I'll tell you what's coming. I'll tell you what Bible experts have to say about it. But you're in the driver's seat. I'll not be telling you what to do about the road ahead.

I will ride along with you, though, to keep you company.

Shotgun.

Buckle up.

Stephen M. Miller
StephenMillerBooks.com

1

A Virgin and a 50-Shekel Fine

If a Jewish man raped a virgin who wasn't engaged, or if he seduced her into having sex, Deuteronomy 22:29 said he had to...

- Pay a fine to her father: 50 silver shekels (1¼ pounds, or 570 grams). That's about the weight of 2½ rolls of quarters or a jeans pocket full of euros.

- Marry her.

- Never divorce her.

It sounds like a cheap way to get a wife, but it was no bargain. It was the value of a man—50 shekels was the price to free a male slave; 30 shekels freed a woman (Leviticus 27:3-4).

It also sounds unfair to force a woman to marry her rapist or her seducer. But the law's intent, some scholars say, was to provide for the woman who otherwise might never have found a husband. In that time and culture, men looking for a wife considered non-virgin single ladies to be damaged goods. Even King David's daughter Tamar never seemed to find a husband after her half brother raped her. She moved out of the palace accommodations for royal virgins and lived with her full brother Absalom "as a desolate woman" (2 Samuel 13:20).

By law, Jewish women couldn't divorce men. But men could divorce women for nothing more than "having discovered something wrong with her" (Deuteronomy 24:1). The unhappy husband wrote his wife a letter of divorce and sent her on her way.

But not so in the marriage of a man who raped or seduced a virgin. For that couple, it was "till death do us part."

The word used in the original Hebrew language to describe the rape is actually a broader word. It's closer to *coercion,* most scholars say. That could imply rape, seduction, or harassment and badgering—as in, "If you really loved me…"

2

Hairy Getaway

The militia of Israel's future king, David, attacked a raiding party of invading nomads, killing all of them except "400 young men who fled on camels" (1 Samuel 30:17).

Upload that as an Internet video, and it would go viral. Imagine 400 bad guys jumping on camels and plodding off into the night—a thundering, thumping getaway in long-legged slow motion.

Some might wonder, "Why not just run?"

Camels are faster. In a short burst, they can zip 40 mph (64 kph). That's about twice as fast as a top Olympic sprinter, or about as fast as your average Eagle Scout on the run from a skunk.

3

Ghostwalker

"It's a ghost!" (Matthew 14:26).

That's what Jesus's disciples screamed when they saw something walking toward them—on the water, during a storm, at three in the morning—while they were rowing for their lives, "fighting heavy waves" (verse 24).

Many Jews believed in ghosts. These Jews may have figured they had lost their battle against the storm and the ghost was coming to take them into the afterlife.

This wasn't the only time the disciples mistook Jesus for a ghost. When he showed up after his crucifixion, "the whole group was startled and frightened, thinking they were seeing a ghost!" (Luke 24:37).

A ghost actually visited King Saul. It came the night before Saul's doomed battle with the Philistines. The spirit of the dead prophet Samuel appeared with depressing news: "Tomorrow... you and your sons will be here with me" (1 Samuel 28:19). That story—famous among the Jews—might explain why the rowing disciples weren't happy about seeing a spirit approaching them like a rogue wave.

4

Fatal Phonetics

A hill-country accent cost 42,000 Jews their lives. They dropped their *h*'s—a bit like some British folks do today. "If I had a hammer" becomes "If I 'ad a 'ammer."

One Jewish hero back in the days of Samson and Gideon took advantage of this accent. He used it to target his enemies—Jews from the tribe of Ephraim, in the hills of central Israel. His name was Jephthah. He hated Ephraimites because they refused to join his militia and help him fight off an enemy in what is now the Arab country of Jordan.

Jephthah captured a shallow ford that travelers used to cross the Jordan River (they didn't have bridges back then). He charged an unusual toll—travelers had to pronounce the word *Shibboleth*.

No one today seems to know what that word meant. It was a tongue-twister for Jews from Ephraim. Most couldn't pronounce it. They died trying. The closest they could get was *Sibboleth* (Judges 12:6).

5

Moses Takes the Scenic Route

Moses and the Exodus Jews took 40 years to make a two-week trip. "Normally it takes only eleven days to travel from Mount Sinai to Kadesh-barnea" (Deuteronomy 1:2).

Mount Sinai, in Egypt's Sinai Peninsula, is where Moses and the Jews camped for about a year after crossing the Red Sea. That's where Moses organized the 12 tribes into a nation with the laws he said God had given him.

Kadesh is an oasis near Israel's southern border, in what is now Egypt. This is where many scholars say Moses and the Jews spent most of their 40-year sentence.

God had sentenced them to 40 years in the badlands because they couldn't muster a speck of faith in spite of all the miracles they had seen God do for them. They refused to invade what is now Israel after their scouts came back with warnings about walled cities and giants.

God decided the invasion could wait for Generation Two.

In fact, the only two adults from Exodus Generation One who lived long enough to step foot on the Promised Land were Joshua and Caleb. They were the two scouts who had recommended that the Jews invade in spite of the walled cities and giants (Deuteronomy 1:36,38).

6

How to Get Rid of House Mold

Get rid of the house. That was the Jewish law of last resort when it came to dealing with mold inside a house.

Before going that far, Jewish law suggested less vigorous remedies under the supervision of a priest.

- Quarantine the house for seven days.
- If the mold remains, remove the part of the house where the mold is growing and then scrape the walls on the rest of the house.

If the mold returns, the house "must be torn down, and all its stones, timbers, and plaster must be carried out of town" (Leviticus 14:45).

> The Hebrew word for *mold* was actually the same word often translated *leprosy*—as though the house had a serious skin disease.

7

Solomon, King of Cheapskates

To build Israel's first temple and a new palace, King Solomon imported top-grade lumber—rot-resistant cedars of Lebanon.

King Hiram of Tyre, a city in what is now Lebanon, had the timber tied into rafts and floated down the seacoast to Israel. He also sent about four and a half tons of gold, perhaps to decorate the walls. That's about the weight of two Cadillacs, fully loaded.

These supplies came dirt cheap to the Jews. Literally and

figuratively. Solomon literally paid Hiram in land. "He gave twenty towns in the land of Galilee to King Hiram" (1 Kings 9:11). That was along the border between the two nations.

When Hiram later inspected the land, he figuratively named it Cabul—apparently an unhappy pun because this name sounds like the Hebrew word for *worthless*. Josephus, a Jewish writer (AD 37–100), said the word meant "unfruitful" in Hiram's Phoenician language.

8

Jewish Entitlements

Jewish law built in some safety nets for people at high risk—folks most likely to get exploited: orphans, widows, the poor, and immigrants.

Here's one. "When you harvest the crops of your land, do not harvest the grain along the edges of your fields, and do not pick up what the harvesters drop. Leave it for the poor and the foreigners living among you. I am the LORD your God" (Leviticus 23:22).

9

Lions Refuse to Eat a Vegetarian

Daniel—of the lion's den fame—was a vegan.

In a touch of irony, those lions—well-established carnivores—refused to dine on him when they had the chance (Daniel 6). As though they became temporary vegans too.

Daniel was a young Jewish noble taken captive to what is now Iraq. There, because of his smarts, he landed a gig in the palace. He served as one of many advisors to the king. So did three of his friends—Shadrach, Meshach, and Abednego, the young Jews who would later survive a visit inside a blazing furnace (Daniel 3:19-30).

Daniel and his buddies were all kosher Jews. They observed Jewish food laws. If they ate meat, it had to be prepared according to Jewish law. No pink steaks, for example, because Jewish law said all blood belonged to God—it was reserved for use in sacrifices (Leviticus 17:10-12).

"Daniel was determined not to defile himself by eating the food and wine given to them by the king" (Daniel 1:8). Rather than risk eating non-kosher meat, he and his friends ate only veggies. As a result, they "looked healthier and better nourished than the young men who had been eating the food assigned by the king" (Daniel 1:15).

10

Don't Call Him Bunny

Bunni (bun-EYE). That was the name of one of the Jewish leaders who helped rebuild Israel after Babylonian invaders (from present-day Iraq) crushed the nation and leveled the capital city of Jerusalem.

English translations spell the Hebrew name as Bunni (Nehemiah 10:15). Some Bible experts say it's a nickname for Benaiah. The name means "God has made," as in "God made a woman [Eve] from the rib, and he brought her to the man [Adam]" (Genesis 2:22).

11

Killer Sermon

Big mistake sitting on a third-story windowsill during a candlelight sermon.

"[Paul] kept talking until midnight…Paul spoke on and on" (Acts 20:8-9). A young man named Eutychus perched himself on the windowsill like a brick bird. He got drowsy. Then he got dead. "He fell sound asleep and dropped three stories to his death" (verse 9).

That's one way to stop a preacher from talking. Drop dead right there in front of him.

Paul went downstairs and revived Eutychus.

Then Paul started up again, preaching until dawn. Either Paul couldn't take a hint, or he had a lot of important things to say. In fact, he was on his way home to Jerusalem after his third and last-reported mission trip. He told another group a short time later that God's Spirit had alerted him that he was headed to jail and suffering. "None of you to whom I have preached the kingdom will ever see me again" (Acts 20:25).

12

Killer Granny

Ahaziah, king of the southern Jewish nation of Judah, managed to get himself murdered while on a horribly timed visit to the northern Jewish nation of Israel—during a coup. When his mom, Queen Mother Athaliah, found out about this, she morphed into a killer granny. "She began to destroy the rest of the royal family" (2 Kings 11:1).

Athaliah came from bad stock as "one of Ahab's daughters"

(2 Kings 8:18). Perhaps her mom was Jezebel, the queen of mean who had tried to kill all God's prophets.

Sadly for Athaliah, she missed killing one baby grandson: Joash. The queen's sis—clearly a soft touch when it came to babies—rushed Joash to the temple, where priests hid him for six years. Then, with the cooperation of palace guards who apparently had their fill of the queen, the high priest anointed young Joash king of Israel.

Soldiers gave the queen a taste of her own brand of mercy. They killed her.

With crowds cheering, the queen died in what amounts to a barnyard—"where horses enter the palace grounds" (2 Kings 11:16).

13

Jews on the Giving End of a Holocaust

Even some of the most God-loving Bible scholars struggle with the marching orders Moses gave Joshua and the Exodus Jews: "Destroy every living thing" (Deuteronomy 20:16).

One exception—plants, which the Jews would need when they took over the land (verses 19-20). But they were to kill all the locals and their animals.

Some scholars choke not only on the order but also on the reason Moses gave to justify it. "This will prevent the people of the land from teaching you to imitate their detestable customs in the worship of their gods, which would cause you to sin deeply against the LORD your God" (verse 18). For many believers, the order seems harsh—even if the Canaanites practiced infant sacrifice and temple prostitution, as some scholars speculate they did.

The Israelites failed to do as Moses ordered. "They took

possession of the hill country. But they failed to drive out the people living in the plains" (Judges 1:19). As a result, Moses's prediction came true. "Instead, the people...moved in among the Canaanites" (verse 32) and learned to live with them as neighbors.

As Moses had warned, the Jews picked up Canaanite religion, worshipping idols. Some Jewish kings even sacrificed their children. "Manasseh also sacrificed his own son in the fire" (2 Kings 21:6).

14
Jewish Orphan Stops a Holocaust

Persia's number two leader—Haman, who reported only to the king—decided to purify the Iranian-based Persian Empire by killing all its Jews.

Why? Because one Jew had refused to bow when he walked by. So kill them all.

That one Jew was Mordecai. He had raised his orphaned cousin until she became Queen Esther. Haman didn't seem to know that Esther was a Jew.

When Esther came storming out of the closet, announcing to the king that she was as Jewish as a matzo ball, the king hanged Haman (Esther 7:10). Then he gave Mordecai Haman's job—a bit like twisting the dagger in a dead guy.

Jews still celebrate this holocaust missed. It's a springtime, Mardi Gras–style holiday called Purim.

15

Why the Good Die Young

Ever wonder why our favorite relatives and friends often seem to die first, leaving us with the Grinch who stole Christmas, Cruella de Vil, and the Wicked Witch of the West?

Conventional Christian wisdom might explain it this way. God wants sweet people first, for the Sweet By-and-By. When it comes to sour souls, heaven can wait. The prophet Isaiah, however, didn't explain it that way. Here's his take.

> Good people pass away;
>   the godly often die before their time.
>   But no one seems to care or wonder why.
> No one seems to understand
>   that God is protecting them from the evil to come.
> For those who follow godly paths
>   will rest in peace when they die (Isaiah 57:1-2).

16

Is the Antichrist an End-Time Myth?

Some Bible experts say yes. They say John was the only Bible writer to use the word *antichrist*, and it never appears in the book of Revelation. He didn't use it to talk about some future beastly demagogue. He used it to describe people in his day who were anti everything Jesus stood for.

- "You have heard that the Antichrist is coming, and already many such antichrists have appeared" (1 John 2:18).

- "Anyone who denies the Father and the Son is an antichrist" (verse 22).

Some Bible historians say the idea of a future, end-time antichrist began to emerge several centuries after Jesus. They say Christian preachers started connecting disconnected passages, piecing them together like a Frankenstein. They linked John's antichrist with the "man of lawlessness" that Paul said was coming and then with the beast of Revelation (2 Thessalonians 2:3-4; Revelation 13:1-8).

Other Christians say John didn't limit the antichrist to his era and that his description of people who were anti Jesus tracks nicely with future beastly leaders predicted in Paul's letters and in Revelation (1 John 4:3; 2 John 1:7).

17

Rome's Mark of the Beast

Revelation, the last book in the Bible, features two hideous beasts. The first comes from the sea. The second comes from the earth. Many Bible experts link Roman emperor Nero to Revelation's beast of the earth for several reasons. Here are two of the biggies.

- "He exercised all the authority of the first beast" (Revelation 13:12).

The first beast came from the sea and had seven heads, which "represent the seven hills of the city" (Revelation 13:1; 17:9). Rome was built on seven hills, and Romans invaded the Jewish homeland by sea. The man who exercised all authority over Rome was the emperor.

- "Let the one with understanding solve the meaning of the number of the beast, for it is the number of a man. His number is 666" (Revelation 13:18).

Roman coins in circulation at the time included some stamped with pictures of Nero and his name, Nero Caesar. Each letter had number values. When you add up the numbers that Jews used to spell Nero Caesar, as translated from Greek, the international language of the day, the total was 666. When you add up the numbers they used to translate it from Latin, the language of Rome, the total was 616—a number that shows up in some ancient copies of Revelation.

On the other hand, many Christians say John wasn't talking just about history. They say he was warning about a future beastly leader—a kindred spirit of Nero who would target Christians.

18

Out-of-Body Traveler

Elisha the prophet had what appears to have been an out-of-body experience after he healed a Syrian commander, Naaman, of a skin disease.

Most English translations of the Bible call the disease leprosy. But scholars say it could have been any number of skin aliments because medical diagnosis wasn't what you'd call precise in the 800s BC.

Naaman brought gifts for Elisha—10 sets of clothing, 750 pounds (340 kg) of silver, and 150 pounds (68 kg) of gold. Elisha politely refused the gift, and Naaman left.

Elisha's servant, Gehazi, saw an opportunity to profit from the prophet. He caught up with Naaman on the road and said

Elisha had changed his mind. He said the prophet would accept 75 pounds (34kg) of silver and two sets of clothing.

Done deal.

When Gehazi got home, Elisha told him, "Don't you realize that I was there in spirit when Naaman stepped down from his chariot to meet you?" (2 Kings 5:26). Gehazi left the room with skin flaked white in leprosy.

Jesus talked as if he had a similar out-of-body experience when he saw his future disciple Nathanael under a distant fig tree (John 1:48).

19

Temporarily Dead

Raiders from what is now Jordan invaded Israel each spring to steal the harvest. These raiders stormed into one field just as some Jews were burying a man.

This was sometime after the prophet Elisha had died and was buried nearby.

Quickly, the burial party tossed the corpse into Elisha's tomb and took off running for their lives.

The dead man joined them. "As soon as the body touched Elisha's bones, the dead man revived and jumped to his feet!" (2 Kings 13:21).

The writer doesn't say if the raiders caught him and killed him. We're left guessing. And hoping he got away.

20

God Kills 70,000 Jews for One Man's Sin

It may seem more devilish than divine, but the Bible says God ordered 70,000 Jews to their death merely because King David took a census (1 Chronicles 21:1-17).

Census results—1,100,000 warriors in Israel. As the writer reports it, God was livid for some unknown reason. Here are two popular theories about why God was angry.

- The census was David's way of taking credit for his military victories instead of giving God credit.

- David neglected to collect the required census tax for the worship center. "Pay me for their lives at the time they are counted. Then a plague will not come" (Exodus 30:12 NIRV).

God gave David three options for punishment: three years of drought, three months of enemy attacks, or three days of plague. David chose the plague, and 70,000 people died as a result.

21

Raiders of the Lost Ark

Nearly 2600 years before film director Steven Spielberg spun a story about the American government hiring archaeologist Indiana Jones to find the Ark of the Covenant before the Nazis got to it, the Ark turned up missing.

Jews had crafted the gold-plated chest in the days of Moses and used it to store the sacred tablets engraved with the Ten Commandments. They kept the Ark in the holiest room in their worship centers—a portable tent during the Exodus travels, and later a permanent temple that King Solomon built in Jerusalem.

Iraqi-based Babylon became the world's bad-boy superpower in 612 BC by crushing the Assyrian army. Like the Assyrians before them, the Babylonians bullied the Middle East, which included the Jewish homeland. When Jews refused to pay the tax Babylon imposed on them, Babylonian king Nebuchadnezzar came to collect.

"Nebuchadnezzar carried away all the treasures from the LORD's Temple and the royal palace. He stripped away all the gold objects that King Solomon of Israel had placed in the Temple" (2 Kings 24:13).

22

A Toddler Named Tragedy

Ephraim, the father of one of Israel's 12 tribes, had three sons. Two were rustlers. They got themselves killed when they tried to steal livestock. Tragic.

Sometime later, Ephraim's wife gave him another son. Ephraim was still in mourning for his two dead sons. Perhaps in their memory, he named his newborn "Beriah because of the tragedy his family had suffered" (1 Chronicles 7:23).

Beriah sounds like *bera'ah*, a Hebrew word that works for *tragedy*, *disaster*, *trouble*, and similar nouns most of us wouldn't have wanted our mother calling us when she tucked us into bed at night.

"Happy dreams, my little Disaster."

23
Israel's Founding Father, the Heel

Folks in Bible times occasionally gave their kids names that had something to do with the circumstances of their birth. Some folks still do that—April was born in April, Harry was hairy, and Joy brought happiness to a previously infertile couple.

Jacob was born holding onto the heel of his twin brother. The Bible says that's why his parents gave him the Hebrew name *Ya 'aqov*, which sounds like the Hebrew word for *heel*—*'aqev* (Genesis 25:26).

Given the early part of his story as a young man, Jacob still seems like a fitting name. He was a heel of a human who set the morality bar lower than a worm's wiggle. He exploited his brother's hunger to get a bigger cut of the family estate, and later he used his elderly father's blindness to steal the deathbed blessing intended for Esau (Genesis 25:27-34; 27).

24
Hell—a Picnic in the Park?

Many people are surprised to learn that hell is a walk in the park today. Literally. It's a beautiful Jerusalem park where folks enjoy picnics and even horseback rides.

Hell is the word most English Bibles use to translate the name of Hinnom Valley (Joshua 15:8; Matthew 5:22). The valley is just south of the 500-year-old walls surrounding the Old City of Jerusalem. Bible translators use the judgment-style word *hell* because the valley name took on a symbolic meaning for the Jews after 586 BC. That's when Babylonian invaders from what is now Iraq leveled Jerusalem and dismantled the Jewish nation.

Jews used the name of the valley to symbolize God's judgment—a bit like Americans use 9/11 as a symbol for the terrorist attacks on New York City and Washington DC.

Jews had apparently worshipped idols in Hinnom Valley, and at least two kings—Ahaz and his grandson Manasseh—even sacrificed their own children (2 Kings 16:3; 21:6). Jews said it was because of sins like these that God punished the Jewish nation by sending Babylonian invaders who leveled Jerusalem and deported most of the surviving Jews.

Bible experts today disagree over what hell is like or even if it exists. Some say...

- It's a real place of eternal torment and physical fire.

- It's a symbol of separation from God. What we wanted in life, we get in the afterlife.

- It's a symbol of annihilation. Just as fire destroys objects, God's judgment will destroy evil souls.

25

Cannibal Cooking

Imprisoned in walled cities surrounded by enemy armies, starving Jews sometimes ate each other.

Not kosher.

Bible writers reported it happening in Jerusalem, capital of the south Jewish nation of Judah.

> Tenderhearted women
>   have cooked their own children.
> They have eaten them
>   to survive the siege (Lamentations 4:10).

It happened in Samaria, too, capital of the northern Jewish nation of Israel. In Samaria, one mother said to another, "Come on, let's eat your son today, then we will eat my son tomorrow" (2 Kings 6:28).

They ate the boy. But then the mother who came up with the idea hid her son. The next day, the besieging army returned home to Syria.

That mom could have nicknamed her son *Mazel Tov*—Hebrew for *good luck*—as in Lucky. Jews today say those Hebrew words at weddings to convey congratulations.

26

To the Jealous Husband: Cheers

In ancient Israel, men got a free pass if their wives suspected them of adultery. (Women didn't.) If a husband merely suspected his wife of having an affair, he could take her to the priest for what some scholars call the "test of the bitter water."

The priest would tell the woman, "If you have been faithful to your husband, this water won't harm you. But if you have been unfaithful, it will bring down the LORD's curse—you will never be able to give birth to a child, and everyone will curse your name" (Numbers 5:19-20 CEV).

The woman would reply, "If I am guilty, let it happen just as you say."

The priest then got a container of holy water, perhaps from one of the basins that held water for sacrificial rituals. He wrote the curse he had spoken onto a scroll and then scraped the ink into the water. He added some dirt from the floor of the worship center (during the Exodus, when this law was drafted, this was a tent).

The woman drank the muddy cocktail.

If she was able to have children afterward, that was to serve as an indication that her husband's suspicions were unfounded.

27

Armageddon: A Battle Not in the Bible?

Here's how the apostle John described Armageddon: "Demonic spirits gathered all the rulers and their armies to a place with the Hebrew name *Armageddon*" (Revelation 16:16). End of story. Period.

That's all John said about *Armageddon*, a word that hasn't turned up in any other ancient lit. Many Bible experts say it's a compound word—*Har Megiddo*, Hebrew for "Mountain of Megiddo."

Megiddo was a fortress that guarded the main pass through the Carmel Mountains in northern Israel. The fort city overlooked the sprawling Jezreel Valley, sometimes called the Valley of Armageddon. Scores of battles have been fought there throughout the centuries.

Many students of the Bible have linked Armageddon to several visions of battles that John reported in other chapters in Revelation. Other scholars say it's hard to tell whether the links are intended as references to the Battle of Armageddon. For example...

- "The number of troops on horseback was 200,000,000" (Revelation 9:16 NIRV).

- "The blood turned into a river that was about two hundred miles long and almost deep enough to cover a horse" (Revelation 14:20 CEV).

28

When the Bible Calls God "Satan"

When we hear the word *Satan*, most of us think of the devil. But if Bible scholars translated that Hebrew word literally, we'd be saying *accuser*, or something similar: *opponent, enemy, adversary.* That's what the word means.

In fact, sometimes the good guys are satans—in this case, an angel: "God's anger was aroused because he went, and the Angel of the Lord took His stand in the way as an adversary [satan] against him" (Numbers 22:22 NKJV).

Even God is described this way. Compare these two versions of the same story:

- "Satan rose up against Israel and caused David to take a census of the people of Israel" (1 Chronicles 21:1).

- "The anger of the Lord burned against Israel, and he caused David to harm them by taking a census" (2 Samuel 24:1).

So when Bible experts read *Satan* in the Bible, they need to take some clues from the context to determine who the writer was talking about.

29

Feeding-Trough Bed: Baby Safe

Luke, a first-century physician who most Bible experts say wrote the Gospel of Luke, describes the birth of Jesus in more detail than any other Gospel writer. As we might expect from a doc.

Luke writes that after Jesus was born, "[Mary] wrapped him

in large strips of cloth. Then she placed him in a manger" (Luke 2:7 NIRV). Or, as the New Century Version translates it, "a feeding trough."

Another first-century physician, Roman writer Soranus, wrote a book called *On Midwifery and the Diseases of Women*. In it, he recommended "swaddling" a baby in tight strips of cloth and using a manger for a crib. He said the swaddling clothes "serve to give firmness and an undistorted figure." He recommended mothers swaddle their baby for 40 to 60 days.

He also said that small feeding troughs made excellent cradles because they were usually tilted, apparently to make it easier for the animals to eat the hay. Mothers could use that tilt to elevate the baby's head, making it easier for the baby to breathe and less likely for it to choke.

30
When Patience Runs Dry

Most folks who know the story of Job think of him as a patient man. That's because he lost just about everything except his faith in God. He lost...

- His children. A windstorm collapsed the house where they were having a party.
- His massive herds, along with the herders.
- His health. Boils erupted all over his body.

To his credit, he never stopped talking to God. But he had his moments—times when his patience ran out and he asked questions any normal God-lover would ask, given the bleak situation: "Does it make you happy when you crush me?" (Job 10:3 NIRV).

Once he went so far as to say, "You, God, are the reaseon I am insulted and spit on" (Job 17:6 CEV).

31
A Drop-Dead Donation to the Church

When the Christian movement got its jump start in Jerusalem, a man named Joseph sold some of his property and donated all of the money to the apostles "to give to those in need" (Acts 4:35). The apostles—Jesus's disciples—were so impressed that they nicknamed the man Barnabas, which means Son of Encouragement.

Perhaps it was "praise envy" that motivated Ananias and Sapphira to do the same. But instead of giving all the proceeds to the apostles, they kept part of it. That would have been fine, but then they lied about it, saying they were donating everything.

Peter met with them individually, accusing them of lying to God. Each one died on the spot. Perhaps of shock—the Bible doesn't say. Most Bible experts say that the context of the story suggests God killed them, or at least that the writer believed God did.

If God did kill them, and his intent was to teach others in this emerging movement that they'd better not toy with him or his servants, it certainly had that effect: "The whole church and, in fact, everyone who heard of these things had a healthy respect for God. They knew God was not to be trifled with" (Acts 5:11 MSG).

32

Drought-Proof Desert Country

Most of the Middle East is plenty dry under normal circumstances. So when Mother Nature added droughts that lasted a year or longer, it was time for herders to go shopping for water and grazing pasture.

One river that never dried up was the Nile, in Egypt (Genesis 45:9-11). It was fed by sources such as Lake Victoria, deep in the heart of Central Africa. The Bible and other ancient reports—including some royal documents from Egypt—tell of refugees bringing their herds and flocks to the grasslands alongside the Nile. Here is an excerpt from a papyrus dating to Old Testament times:

> We have finished letting the Bedouin tribes of Edom [modern-day Jordan] pass the Fortress of Mernepthah...to keep them alive and to keep their cattle alive.*

That's how the Jews ended up in slavery there.

During a seven-year drought, Jacob moved his family to Goshen, "the best land of Egypt" (Genesis 47:11). That's where the Nile fans out into a wide wedge of streams that empty into the Mediterranean Sea.

Jacob's descendants overstay their welcome. A later king of Egypt saw their growing numbers as a threat: "There are way too many of these Israelites for us to handle. We've got to do something: Let's devise a plan to contain them, lest if there's a war they should join our enemies" (Exodus 1:9-10 MSG).

Only after God sent Moses and ten plagues did the king set them free.

---

* Papyrus 10245, Anastasi VI, from the New Kingdom (about 1550–1070 BC), on display in the British Museum.

33

Judas: Jesus's Treasurer

Judas was the money guy for the disciples—the keeper of the stash they used to cover their expenses.

Jesus apparently accepted donations. Luke said a group of women were among his big supporters. They included Mary Magdalene and Joanna, wife of the man who managed the finances of Herod Antipas, Galilee's ruler and the son of Herod the Great. "These women used their own money to help Jesus and his apostles" (Luke 8:3 NCV).

Judas kept it in his little box of goodies. But as John reported, "He was a thief...the one who kept the money box, and he often stole from it" (John 12:6 NCV).

John said that was why Judas complained about Mary of Bethany pouring a 12-ounce (327 g) jar of perfume onto Jesus: "Why wasn't this perfume sold? Why wasn't the money given to poor people? It was worth a year's pay" (verse 5 NIRV).

In other words, John said Judas was really thinking, "Why isn't that money in my money box?" He handled all expenses, including charitable donations. Especially to his favorite charity—himself.

34

Unforgivable: Dissing the Holy Spirit

Pastors have said this is one of the most persistent worries their parishioners have—they think they've committed the unforgivable sin. Their worry comes from this sound bite, part of a conversation Jesus had with Jewish scholars: "Every sin and blasphemy can be forgiven—except blasphemy against the Holy Spirit, which will never be forgiven" (Matthew 12:31).

So folks worry that if they've cussed out the Holy Spirit a good one or said something else that belongs on the flip side of a compliment, they're doomed. But Bible experts agree that those worrying folks have nothing to worry about. They point to Bible verses like these:

- "He forgives all my sins" (Psalm 103:3).
- "If we confess our sins to God, he can always be trusted to forgive us and take our sins away" (1 John 1:9 CEV).

That said, Bible experts are still perplexed by what Jesus said. Given the context of the sound bite—Jesus responding to scholars who said he got his power from the devil instead of God—Bible experts offer theories about what Jesus meant by "blasphemy against the Holy Spirit."

One of their favorite theories: refusing to believe in Jesus, which is where the Jewish scholars were. If we don't believe what Jesus taught about sin, confession, and forgiveness, then we don't confess our sins. And if we don't confess our sins, we don't get forgiven.

On the other hand, if we do confess, here's the promise from God himself: "No matter how deep the stain of your sins, I can take it out and make you as clean as freshly fallen snow. Even if you are stained as red as crimson, I can make you white as wool!" (Isaiah 1:18 TLB).

35
Solomon's Mom: King David's Mistress

King Solomon was not a bastard in the legal sense. But his older brother was.

Solomon's older brother was conceived by a man and a woman who weren't married to each other. They were married to other people.

His father was King David, married to an estimated seven other wives at the time of the affair. His mother was Bathsheba, married to one of David's elite warriors, Uriah, who was off fighting a war in what is now Jordan.

In one of the most famous scenes in the Bible, David saw Bathsheba taking an afternoon bath. He invited her to his place. They had sex. She got pregnant (2 Samuel 11:2-5). The Bible writer doesn't say whether Bathsheba was a willing lover or merely a compliant servant of the alpha male.

The writer probably didn't know. It's not the kind of thing you'd generally ask. "Your Highness, did Bathsheba really want to have sex with you?"

David ordered Bathsheba's husband to come home, hoping Uriah would have sex with her and think the baby was his. Uriah didn't, so David sent him on a suicide mission and married the grieving widow.

Bathsheba gave birth to a boy who lived for only a week (2 Samuel 12:18). Sometime later, "David comforted Bathsheba, his wife, and slept with her. She became pregnant and gave birth to a son, and they named him Solomon" (verse 24).

36
Temple: Occupied

Jehu was one crafty soldier who knew how to get people dead.

He commanded a chariot corps along Israel's northeast border with Syria until the prophet Elisha anointed him as Israel's future king. Feeling God's blessing, right away Jehu led his men on a 40 mile (64 km) charge to Jezreel, summer getaway city of the current king, Ahab's son Joram. There, Jehu assassinated the king and the infamous queen mother, Jezebel. For good measure, Jehu ordered the heads of all the king's potential heirs.

Jehu also wanted to get rid of Jezebel's preferred religion, the worship of the Canaanite god Baal. He put out this fib of a message: "King Ahab sometimes worshiped Baal, but I will be completely faithful to Baal. I'm going to offer a huge sacrifice to him. So invite his prophets and priests, and be sure everyone who worships him is there. Anyone who doesn't come will be killed" (2 Kings 10:18-19 CEV).

Bait and switch. Everyone who came got killed.

Jehu had 80 soldiers hiding near the temple. When the Baal worshippers started their rituals, the soldiers started theirs. No survivors. Soldiers destroyed the temple.

Locals—in what sounds like a nose-holding editorial comment on Jezebel and her religion—turned the site from a place of bowing to a place of squatting. "They completely destroyed Baal's temple. And since that time, it's been nothing but a public toilet" (verse 27 CEV).

37

Baldy's Bear Revenge

Shortly after the prophet Elijah was carried into the sky by a whirlwind, his protégé, Elisha, was walking to Bethel, a village about a dozen miles (19 km) north of Jerusalem.

A gang of boys started jeering him: "Get out of here, baldy!" (2 Kings 2:23 TNIV). Actually, "Get out of here" is phrased a bit like it's a reference to Elijah getting carried away. Another way of translating the phrase is "Go up too, you bald head!" (NCV). The boys could have been saying, "Drop dead."

"Elisha…put a curse on them in the name of the LORD" (verse 24 NCV). Two bears charged the boys and tore 42 of them to pieces.

It seems harsh to kill children for what children do best, which is taunt and tease. Yet the Bible doesn't say God is the one who sent the bears to kill the kids. It could have been a coincidence. But most scholars say that the writer probably connected the two because Jews in Bible times often taught that whatever took place happened on God's watch. He was responsible.

Some Christians would say the story was exaggerated as it was passed along by word of mouth before it was written down and put in the Bible. Other Christians wouldn't take kindly to that theory. They argue that Bible stories like these are historically accurate.

38

A Prophet Gives Mouth-to-Mouth CPR

An elderly couple showed the prophet Elisha hospitality by providing a guest room for him. In response, Elisha offered to grant them a wish.

The lady of the house wished for a son. Elisha said that within a year she would have a boy. Her wish came true, but a few years later the boy suddenly died.

The only clue about how he died is that he was going into the field to see his father during harvest. He cried out, "My head! My head!" (2 Kings 4:19 GWT). One guess is that he died of heatstroke. It can cause headaches.

Servants carried the boy back home, where he died in his mother's arms. The mother saddled a donkey and went to Mount Carmel to bring Elisha back to revive her son.

"He lay on the boy, putting his mouth on the boy's mouth, his eyes on the boy's eyes, his hands on the boy's hands. He crouched over the boy's body, and it became warm" (verse 34 GWT).

39

Waiting for Elijah's Big Comeback

Elijah left the planet in a whirlwind.

To some readers, the Bible's description sounds like a tornado in a thunderstorm. As Elijah and his apprentice prophet Elisha were walking, "a fiery chariot with fiery horses separated the two of them, and Elijah went to heaven in a windstorm" (2 Kings 2:12 GWT).

Remarkable exit. It boosted Elijah into the top ten of who's who in Jewish history—alongside the likes of Noah, Abraham, Moses, and David.

Elijah got an added boost some 400 years later when the prophet Malachi predicted Elijah would come back. "[God] will send you the prophet Elijah. He will come before the day of the LORD arrives" (Malachi 4:5 NIRV).

Since then, some Jews have been anticipating Elijah's arrival as an advance man for the Messiah. Many Jews celebrating the Passover meal will set out an extra cup of wine for Elijah in case he decides to join them and announce that the Messiah has come.

Some also set up a chair for him at circumcision ceremonies. That grew out of an ancient Jewish tradition. Complaining that people weren't obeying God's laws, such as the crucial law about circumcising each baby boy, Elijah said, "I am the only one left" (1 Kings 19:10). Tradition says God assured Elijah that he was wrong, adding, "From now on, Jews will never perform a circumcision without your participation."

The New Testament reports that Elijah did return. Literally and figuratively.

- *Literally.* He appeared with Jesus at the Transfiguration. "Suddenly, Moses and Elijah appeared and began talking with Jesus" (Matthew 17:3).

- *Figuratively.* The angel Gabriel, predicting the birth of John the Baptist, said, "He will be a man with the spirit and power of Elijah" (Luke 1:17).

Years later, Jesus confirmed the fulfillment of the prophecy. "'Elijah has already come, but he wasn't recognized, and they chose to abuse him. And in the same way they will also make the Son of Man suffer.' Then the disciples realized he was talking about John the Baptist" (Matthew 17:12-13).

40

Here's Mud in Your Eye

"[Jesus] spit on the ground, made mud with the saliva, and spread the mud over the blind man's eyes" (John 9:6).

Jesus wasn't the only person in his century treating eye diseases with spit and mud. A similar treatment shows up in a 37-book collection called *Natural History* written by a Roman science writer called Pliny the Elder (AD 27–79).

- "To cure inflammation of the eyes, wash the eyes each morning with spit from your overnight fast."

- "To protect your eyes from developing eye diseases including inflammation of the eyes, do this and you will never again develop an eye disease. Each time you wash the dust off your feet, touch your eyes three times with the muddy water."*

Jesus didn't have to use spit-mud on other occasions. "He touched their eyes and said, 'Because of your faith, it will happen'" (Matthew 9:29). Jesus may have used spit-mud for the one blind man simply to help his faith by using a medical technique familiar to him. At least that's what some biblical scholars speculate.

Saliva does have antibacterial and antiviral properties, making it a natural disinfectant, according to some medical studies. It also moistens dry eyes, helping prevent disease. However, eye docs, such as my son-in-law, Dr. Jonathan Eck, OD, advise against using spit. They recommend more sanitary disinfectants and watering drops that don't have particles from yesterday's burrito mixed into the slobber.

---

* *Remedies from Living Creatures,* book 28, chapter 10

41

Kosher: Surrogate Moms

If a woman could not give her husband a child, ancient Middle Eastern custom allowed her to provide her husband with a surrogate—often a slave girl. Sarah did that, offering Abraham her maid, Hagar, who gave Abraham the son Ishmael (Genesis 16). Later, Rachel and Leah offered Jacob their maids to their husband, Jacob (Genesis 29:31–30:13).

Laws about this show up in ancient contracts, such as this one from the town of Nuzi, in what is now Iraq:

> If Gilimninu [wife] fails to bear children, Gilimninu shall get for Shennima [husband] a woman from the Lullu country as concubine [a slave girl]. In that case, Gilimninu will have authority over the child that is born.

Jewish law says nothing about surrogate mothers. But it does presume that some men will have more than one wife, though it never actually condones the practice: "Suppose a man has two wives…" (Deuteronomy 21:15).

Most Bible experts say that God revealed his preference for marriage when he created Adam and Eve—one man with one woman.

42

Did Jesus Only Pretend to Die?

Early Christians didn't all agree on who or what Jesus was. This led to some church splits.

One breakaway group argued that Jesus wasn't human. Scholars call them Docetists—from a Greek word that means "appears" or "seems"—because they taught that Jesus was a spirit being who only seemed to be human and to suffer on the cross, die, and rise from the dead. The apostle John didn't mince any words when describing this group. "These deceitful liars are saying that Jesus Christ did not have a truly human body" (2 John 7 CEV).

Apparently, these Christians were pioneers of a heresy known as Gnosticism, which spread widely throughout the Christian church in the next couple of centuries, threatening the movement. Many Gnostics taught that the spiritual world was good and the physical world was bad. They couldn't handle the idea that the spiritual and physical—divinity and humanity—could coexist in Jesus.

Most church leaders united against Gnosticism. Church councils wrote creeds opposing it and branded it as a heresy.

43

Vicious Empire of Girlie Men

The Jewish prophet Nahum picked out the biggest thug on the block and called him a girl. And not just any girl, but a slut.

"'I am your enemy!' says the LORD of Heaven's Armies. 'And now I will lift your skirts and show all the earth your nakedness and shame'" (Nahum 3:5). In Bible times, this was a common punishment for a prostitute or an adulterous woman. "I will strip her naked in public, while all her lovers look on" (Hosea 2:10).

Nahum was talking about the Assyrian Empire, which man-handled Middle Eastern nations with such terror tactics as impaling captives on sharpened fence posts. In fact, Assyrian royalty considered war scenes like that suitable for framing. Etched in stone, those images hung on the palace walls in Nineveh and have been uncovered by archaeologists. Some are on display in the British Museum in London.

44
Handwriting on the Wall

There's an old saying, "He couldn't see the handwriting on the wall." It comes from a Bible story about Belshazzar, a Babylonian ruler in what is now Iraq. He watched a disembodied hand write a coded message on the wall that included four words: numbered, numbered, weighed, and divided. The prophet Daniel interpreted those four words this way.

Numbered: Your days are numbered.

Numbered: Your number is up.

Weighed: You've been weighed, and you don't measure up to God's standards.

Divided: Your kingdom has been divided between the Persians and the Medes.

Even though the news was bad, Belshazzar was impressed. "At Belshazzar's command, Daniel was dressed in purple robes" (Daniel 5:29). And just in time. "That very night Belshazzar, the Babylonian king, was killed. And Darius the Mede took over the kingdom at the age of sixty-two" (verses 30-31).

Historians have yet to uncover archaeological evidence of anyone named Darius the Mede. Some speculate that this may have been a nickname for Gubaru. Babylonian inscriptions say Cyrus of Persia put Gubaru in charge of the conquered Babylonian territories.

45

Chickenhearted General

For 20 years a Canaanite king had been raiding the Israelites' homeland. He lived in the city-kingdom of Hazor, north of the Sea of Galilee. His army could field a corps of 900 chariots, which produced a battlefield fear factor comparable to tanks today.

The prophetess Deborah told Barak, the general of the Jewish army, to assemble his militia because God told her it was time to stop the invaders.

Apparently, Barak wasn't much of a believer. "Barak said to Deborah... 'if you won't go with me, I won't go'" (Judges 4:8 NCV). Deborah agreed, but she warned him that a woman would get the glory for winning the battle.

Deborah ordered the troops to muster onto the steep slopes of Mount Tabor—a great strategy for defending against chariots. As the chariot corps charged toward them, a rainstorm erupted, trapping the chariots in fields of mud.

Deborah ordered her militia to charge. The invaders abandoned their chariots and ran for their lives.

46

Dictated Prophecy

Most people in Old Testament times couldn't read or write. When they needed to get something down in writing, they hired a professional writer known as a scribe. The prophet Jeremiah used a scribe to write a book in the Bible. "Jeremiah dictated everything that the LORD had told him, and Baruch wrote it all down on a scroll" (Jeremiah 36:4 GWT).

The Bible identifies Jeremiah's scribe as "Baruch son of Neriah" (Jeremiah 32:12). Jeremiah used Baruch's services at least twice. The king didn't like the first draft of Jeremiah's prophecies, so he cut it to pieces and threw it into a fire. Jeremiah dictated a second, expanded edition, including prophecies against the king. This edition is thought to be the one that's now in the Old Testament.

In 1975, archaeologists found a stash of 250 clay impressions. One of them seems to have been made from the seal Baruch used to press his mark onto plugs of soft clay or wax. Scribes used these plugs to seal letters and scrolls and protect the privacy of the contents. A second seal impression turned up in 1996. Both impressions read, "Belonging to Berekyahu son of Neriyahu the scribe." Some scholars speculate that those are the formal names of Baruch and his father. Others say the impressions may be forgeries.

47

Paul's Visit to Paradise

Writing in a letter to Christians at Corinth, Greece, Paul defended his apostleship from people who said he was a fraud. In his defense, Paul talked about the hardships he had suffered and the spiritual experiences that had blessed his life and his ministry.

Among the blessings was one that sounds like either a vision or an out-of-body experience. "Whether I was in my body or out of my body, I don't know—only God knows" (2 Corinthians 12:2). Paul didn't provide a lot of details. All he said about that experience was, "I do know that I was caught up to paradise and heard things so astounding that they cannot be expressed in words, things no human is allowed to tell" (verse 3).

48

Poetry in Motion Stops the Sun

After leading his men on an all-night march from the Jordan River Valley up into the Judean hills to rescue a besieged city, Joshua prayed a remarkable prayer that has left scholars scratching their noggins. "Joshua prayed…'Our LORD, make the sun stop in the sky over Gibeon, and the moon stand still over Aijalon Valley.' So the sun and the moon stopped and stood still until Israel defeated its enemies" (Joshua 10:12-13 CEV).

Many Christians say they believe the sun and moon actually stopped moving in the sky.

Other Christians can't get past the science. Some of those Christians prefer to interpret the prayer as poetry, intended figuratively. The prayer itself was written in the form of poetry. The report that follows, however, indicating the sun and moon actually stopped, is written in prose.

Some scholars say that one approach is to recognize that the Hebrew word for *stopped* doesn't have to mean "stopped moving." It could mean "stopped shining." That works, at least to some degree, because storm clouds rolled in, blocking out the sun and killing most of Joshua's enemies by pummeling them with hailstones.

49

Hosea and the Prostitute: A Match Made in Heaven

God often asked his prophets to act out their prophecies. He once told Ezekiel to shave his head and beard and then destroy the hair. This was to represent the coming destruction of the Jewish nation (Ezekiel 5).

What God asked of Hosea seems, to many souls, over the top—a little too much, and not very godly. "He said to him, 'Go and marry a prostitute.'" The Lord explained why he was asking this of Hosea: "This will illustrate how Israel has acted like a prostitute by turning against the LORD and worshiping other gods" (Hosea 1:2).

Well, yeah, that's a good way to illustrate it. But some wonder, does God have to destroy a prophet's life and the life of his kids in the process?

Most Bible experts in ancient times said they couldn't believe God would ask something like this of a prophet. One theory they came up with is that the story itself is a kind of parable—fiction, to illustrate a point. Another theory is that Hosea experienced all of this in a dream, and that when he woke up he simply reported his nightmare. Yet there's no indication in the book that this story had anything to do with a dream.

50

Grandpa Is My Daddy

Judah's sneaky daughter-in-law Tamar was in need of a son. Her husband had died without leaving her a son to take care of her. That was a big deal. In this patriarchal age, women were not allowed to inherit property. They needed a male figure to look after them.

It was custom for the nearest relative of the deceased husband to marry the widow in an attempt to provide her with a son who could inherit the first husband's property and take care of his mother in her old age.

As leader of the clan, Judah was responsible for providing Tamar with a replacement husband. He provided one sub—another of his sons—who also died. That's where Judah stopped. He refused to give Tamar his third son. He worried that this son might end up dead too.

Tamar maneuvered herself into getting pregnant by Judah. Veiling her face, she pretended to be a hooker. The plan worked, and she had twin boys.

"Judah...had no idea that she was his daughter-in-law" (Genesis 38:15-16 MSG). He never slept with Tamar again.

As a matter of genetics, Judah was the father of the twins. But under the law, he was their grandpa.

51

Incest in the King's House

Crown Prince Amnon fell in lust with his half sister, Princess Tamar. Same father—King David—different mothers.

Amnon pretended to get sick, and asked Tamar to bring him food. When she came in, he raped her. In the afterglow, "Amnon's love turned to hate, and he hated her even more than he had loved her" (2 Samuel 13:14-15).

Tamar, who was considered damaged goods in that culture, moved in with her full brother Absalom. There's no indication she ever got married.

The rape left King David angry, but he did nothing. So Absalom took it upon himself to settle the matter. He invited Amnon to a party. "Absalom told his men, 'Wait until Amnon gets drunk; then at my signal, kill him!'" (verse 28).

After Amnon's murder, bitterness between David and Absalom festered for years. Finally, Absalom led a coup against his father but died in the battle.

52

Father of the Jews Marries His Half Sister

A sex sin gave birth to the Jewish nation.

That's one way to read the Bible history. Abraham fathered the Jewish nation by having sex with his half sister. He explained, "She really is my sister. She's the daughter of my father, but not the daughter of my mother. And she became my wife" (Genesis 20:12 NIRV).

Hear the word of the Lord several centuries later from the lips of Moses the Lawgiver:

- "Don't have sex with any of your close relatives...sister or stepsister...or half sister" (Leviticus 18:6,9,11 CEV).

- "We ask the LORD to put a curse on any man who sleeps with his sister or his half sister" (Deuteronomy 27:22 CEV).

In defense of Abraham, scholars say he wasn't breaking that law because it didn't exist yet. The fact that Abraham married his half sister shows how old the story is, scholars add. Abraham predates Moses and the Jewish laws by more than half a millennium.

In the time of Abraham, around 2100 BC, marrying a half sister apparently wasn't unheard of in the ancient Middle East. There didn't seem to be any laws prohibiting it at the time.

Some Bible experts a few centuries ago didn't care much for the idea that Abraham broke what would become a fairly important Jewish law. One of those scholars was John Calvin (1509–1564), theological father of many Baptists and Presbyterians. Calvin and others argued that Abraham and Sarah were cousins. But most scholars today say that's not what the writer of Genesis said.

53
Arab Mother of the Jews

King David isn't the only reason the story of his great-grandmother Ruth ended up in Scripture, some Bible experts say. In fact, they add, it probably wasn't even the most important reason.

They say that Jewish scholars who signed off on the books that ended up in their Bible, which Christians call the Old Testament, weren't interested merely in tracing the family tree of Israel's most revered line of kings—a dynasty that lasted more than 400 years.

These modern Bible experts say the ancient Jewish scholars

may have seen in Ruth's story a healthy counterpoint to the seemingly harsh command that a priest named Ezra made some 700 years after Ruth: "Divorce your foreign wives" (Ezra 10:11 CEV).

That's exactly what Ruth was—a foreign wife from what is now the Arab country of Jordan. She moved to Bethlehem and married a Jewish farmer named Boaz. "The LORD blessed her with a son [Obed]...When Obed grew up he had a son named Jesse, who later became the father of King David" (Ruth 4:13,17 CEV).

If Boaz would have done what Ezra later ordered all Jewish men to do, Ruth would have moved back to Jordan, taking her baby with her—David's grandfather.

In fairness to Ezra and his seemingly cruel command, the Jews had just returned from exile in what is now Iraq. Some said they believed that one of the main reasons God let them lose their homeland is because they married non-Jews and started worshiping non-Jewish gods. One thousand years earlier, Moses had warned Jews not to marry Canaanites for that very reason: "You must not intermarry with them...for they will lead your children away from me to worship other gods" (Deuteronomy 7:3-4).

However, some scholars say there's no indication in the story that God had anything to do with Ezra's demand. Some add that it's possible the words of Moses were intended for the first generations of Jews getting settled in the Promised Land and not for all Jews for all time.

54

Wise Men Follow a Star

Christians wanting science to explain the Bethlehem star are left wanting. No theory tracks perfectly with a literal read of the story.

Matthew's Gospel says that stargazers from somewhere east of Israel, perhaps Iraq or Iran, saw something in the sky that led them to believe a future king of the Jews had just been born. "The star they had seen in the east guided them to Bethlehem. It went ahead of them and stopped over the place where the child was" (Matthew 2:9).

They arrived in Jerusalem, capital city of the Jews, two years after Jesus was born. That's what a number of scholars conclude from Herod's tactic to prevent anyone from taking his throne: "He sent soldiers to kill all the boys in and around Bethlehem who were two years old and under, based on the wise men's report of the star's first appearance" (verse 16).

The only theory that tracks nicely with the Bible story is one that says the moving light was some kind of a divine manifestation, perhaps like the pillar of fire that led Moses and the Jews out of Egypt.

Another recent theory says the star may have been a conjunction of planets. Jupiter and Saturn appeared to nudge up next to each other inside the Pisces constellation in 7 BC.

- Jupiter was the Roman name for Zeus, king of the gods, so it represented kings.

- Saturn represented Jews because they worshipped on Saturday, the day named after the god Saturn.

- Pisces, meaning "fish," represented the land around the Mediterranean Sea, including the Jewish homeland.

At that time in history, after the Jews had endured several decades of Roman occupation, hopes for a Messiah were at a fever pitch—even among Jews scattered abroad in foreign countries. Knowing about this, the wise men may have figured that the signs in the sky suggested the Messiah had finally come.

<h1 style="text-align:center">55</h1>

What to Do with a Resurrected Man

When we read the account of what happens after Jesus raised Lazarus from the dead, it might sound like the punch line to a racist joke.

What does a Jew do to a man who can raise the dead?

Kill him. And everyone he raised. Happy Passover.

That's what the Bible says the top Jewish leaders decided to do with Jesus and Lazarus on the eve of the year's most celebrated Jewish holiday. "High priests plotted to kill Lazarus because so many of the Jews were going over and believing in Jesus on account of him" (John 12:10-11 MSG).

The story of Lazarus shows up in only the Gospel of John, the one Gospel most devoted to presenting Jesus as not just a human blessed by God but as the divine Son of God.

From John's point of view, Jewish leaders had a choice.

- They could let reality shape their beliefs. Recognizing Jesus as divine, if for no other reason than his ability to perform God-caliber miracles, they could adjust their preconceived notions to match what they've seen with their own eyes.

- Or they could allow tradition to trump reality, clinging to traditional Jewish teaching and destroying all traces of anything that contradicts it.

56

How to Land a Husband

King David's great-grandmother, a widow named Ruth, proposed to her second husband in bed.

Ruth was caring for elderly Naomi, the mother of her deceased husband. Tradition called for the next closest relative to marry the young widow and take care of her—ancient social security. Boaz was not only an eligible relative, he had shown an interest in Ruth—inviting her to eat with him and to take some of his freshly harvested grain for herself.

When Ruth told Naomi about Boaz, Naomi lit up and transfigured into matchmaker mode.

While Boaz was sleeping out in his field, guarding his crops during harvest season, Naomi told Ruth, "Wash yourself. Put on some perfume. And put on your best clothes. Then go down to the threshing floor. But don't let Boaz know you are there. Wait until he has finished eating and drinking. Notice where he lies down. Then go over and uncover his feet. Lie down there. He'll tell you what to do" (Ruth 3:3-4 NIRV).

"After his evening meal, Boaz felt good and went to sleep lying beside the pile of grain. Ruth went to him quietly and lifted the cover from his feet and lay down" (verse 7 NCV). When Boaz, an elderly man, woke up in the middle of the night, there was young Ruth—warming his feet and smelling sweet.

She proposed. The couple married and had a baby—Obed, grandfather of King David.

57

Cain's Mark of Mercy

After Cain, a farmer, polluted the ground with the blood of his brother Abel, whom he murdered, God banished Cain from the farmland.

"When you farm the ground," God told him, "it will no longer yield its best for you. You will be a fugitive, a wanderer on the earth" (Genesis 4:12 GWT).

Cain said that was cruel and unusual punishment. "Now anyone who finds me will kill me!" (verse 14 GWT).

To prevent that, "the LORD put a mark on Cain warning anyone who met him not to kill him" (verse 15 NCV).

The writer never says what the mark was. Some Christians in centuries past speculated it was black skin. Most scholars call that a shot in the dark.

As the Bible tells it, some of Cain's descendants included Africans. But they also included Middle Eastern races, such as the Canaanites who lived in what is now Israel.

58

Flood Cruise

The story of the flood uses an odd calendar to mark its key events, which place Noah, his family, and the critters on the ark for a full year—not just 40 days.

Today, we run our calendar off the birth of Jesus. But this account uses a calendar based on the birth of Noah. Here's the timeline.

- Flood starts on 2.17.600—Noah's six hundredth year, second month, seventeenth day.

- Rain stops on 3.26.600, forty days later.

- Boat grinds to a halt on a mountain in the Ararat range on 7.17.600, five months after the flood started.

- Other mountain peaks are visible on 10.1.600, a little over seven months into the flood.

- Dove sent out on 12.1.600 and doesn't return. About ten months into the flood, the land is dry enough for the bird to land.

- Passengers disembark on 2.27.601, a little over a year after the flood. "Two more months went by, and at last the earth was dry! Then God said to Noah, 'Leave the boat, all of you'" (Genesis 8:14-16).

59
Ganging Up on the Gang Rapists

A group of Jews from the tribe of Benjamin gang-raped to death a Jewish woman passing through their town. It was a bit like the city council raping to death the wife of an evangelist leading revival services at the Baptist church.

"Leading citizens of Gibeah" (Judges 20:5)—King Saul's birthplace, a few miles north of Jerusalem—surrounded the house where a Levite (a priest's assistant) and his concubine (a second-class wife) were spending the night on their journey home. The rapists didn't want the woman. They wanted the Levite.

Not quite the husband who would take a bullet for his beloved, "the Levite grabbed his concubine and forced her outside" (Judges 19:25 GWT). When he found her dead the next morning, he took her corpse home, cut it into 12 pieces, shipped each piece to one of Israel's 12 tribes, and demanded justice.

The Israelites nearly annihilated the tribe of Benjamin, "leaving only 600 men who escaped" (Judges 20:47).

60

Don't Mess with a Girl Who Has 12 Brothers

After the prince of Shechem, a city in what is now Israel, raped Dinah, daughter of Jacob, he fell in love with her and asked to marry her. Her brothers said, "We'll agree, but only on one condition. You will have to become like us. You will have to circumcise all of your males" (Genesis 34:15 NIRV).

Dinah's brothers were thinking ahead. Get the men unfit to fight, then fight them.

Leading the attack were two of Dinah's full brothers, sons of Jacob's first wife, Leah. "Simeon and Levi, two of Dinah's brothers, attacked with their swords and killed every man in town" (Genesis 34:25 CEV). No rapist was going to marry their little sis.

Oddly enough, centuries later Moses would demand that anyone who raped an eligible woman had to marry her (see number 1, "A Virgin and a 50-Shekel Fine").

61

Jesus: Cheers!

In his first reported miracle, Jesus turned enough water into wine to get more than 1000 people too drunk to drive a donkey cart.

He produced no less than 120 gallons, which is enough to fill two or three standard-sized bathtubs: "six stone water jars, used for Jewish ceremonial washing. Each could hold twenty to thirty gallons" (John 2:6).

Here's the math on drunkenness. Start with .08 percent blood alcohol, the US legal measure of a drunken soul. It takes three 5-ounce glasses of wine for the blood level in an average-sized person to hit that mark. That's 15 ounces per person.

Jesus produced more than 15,000 ounces. Enough to get more than 1000 people drunk.

Fortunately, Bible-time weddings lasted for days, sometimes weeks. So people didn't drink the wine all at once. There's no report in the Bible that anyone at this wedding had trouble driving their donkey cart home.

62

Curses on My Grandson

After the great flood, Noah planted a vineyard. Going a little overboard on the wine, "he became drunk and lay naked inside his tent" (Genesis 9:21).

Son number three of three—Ham—saw him and called in his two older brothers to have a look-see. Oddly, when Noah sobered up and heard what Ham did, Noah cursed Ham's apparently innocent son instead of him: "May there be a curse on Canaan! May he be the lowest slave to his brothers" (Genesis 9:25 NCV).

The Bible writer doesn't say why Noah did this. Here are two theories. The curse was...

- *Prophecy.* Israel later defeated the descendants of Canaan, including the Canaanites and the Egyptians.
- *Payback.* Noah wanted to hurt Ham hard. Messing with a father's beloved son would do that.

63

Oh Little Town of Fishermen

Capernaum was a convenient headquarters for at least four of Jesus's disciples: brothers Peter and Andrew, and brothers James and John. All four had worked there as village fishermen. It became Jesus's ministry center of operations. "He left Nazareth and made his home in Capernaum on the shores of the Sea of Galilee" (Matthew 4:13 GWT).

Archaeologists found the ruins of a house that may have belonged to Peter.

A Spanish pilgrim named Lady Egeria, writing in the AD 380s, said she visited the "House of Simon, called Peter." She said the original walls were still standing but that the house had been turned into a church.

The Roman Empire legalized the formerly outlawed Christian religion in the AD 300s. That's when Christians started building churches. Before then, they met mainly in houses.

64

Faith That Amazed Even Jesus

Plenty of people asked Jesus to cure them, and they believed he could do it. But only one man on record said he believed Jesus could heal by long distance—a Roman army officer with a servant paralyzed and in terrible pain.

When Jesus offered to go to the man's house to heal the boy, the officer gave this reply:

> Lord, I am not worthy for you to come into my house. You only need to command it, and my servant will be healed. I, too, am a man under the authority of others, and I have soldiers under my command. I tell one soldier, "Go," and he goes. I tell another soldier, "Come" and he comes (Matthew 8:8-9 NCV).

The soldier may have been showing his awareness of Jewish traditions. Jews became ritually unclean and temporarily unfit to worship God at the temple if they went into the home of a non-Jew. Before they could worship again, they had to go through cleansing rituals.

At any rate, Jesus was impressed. "Jesus...was so surprised that he turned and said to the crowd following him, 'I tell you that in all of Israel I've never found anyone with this much faith!'" (verse 10 CEV).

65
Who Stole John 5:4?

The King James Version and New King James Version are the only translations that include this verse: "An angel went down at a certain time into the pool and stirred up the water; then whoever stepped in first, after the stirring of the water, was made well of whatever disease he had" (John 5:4 NKJV).

Bible experts dropped this verse from most Bible translations for one simple reason: It's not in the oldest and most reliable copies of the Bible.

Back when William Shakespeare was writing plays like *Romeo and Juliet*, Bible scholars in England were translating the Bible into the king's English—a job they finished in 1611. To translate the New Testament, they drew mainly from manuscripts written about a century earlier in Greek and Latin. Since then, scholars have turned up thousands of older copies of the New Testament—some dating back to the AD 100s.

John 5:4 isn't there.

Here's one of many theories about how it ended up in more recent copies of the Bible: An editor read John 5:3 and figured it needed some explanation. "Many sick people were lying on the porches beside the pool. Some were blind, some were crippled, and some were paralyzed" (NCV).

The editor figured readers would want to know what sick folks were doing lying beside the Pool of Bethesda. Tanning? Girl watching? Waiting for a miracle? His suggestion may have started out as a note in the margin, a bit like a footnote. But if it did, it didn't stay there.

Publishers today who produce the King James Version and its update, the New King James Version, have decided to err on the side of preserving this original work of history. Publishers of newer translations try to draw from the latest resources available in an effort to get as close as possible to the original message of the Bible.

66
A Mother-in-Law Worth Keeping

At Jesus's ministry headquarters in the village of Capernaum, he healed a Roman officer's servant who had been paralyzed and in great pain. Then Jesus went to Peter's house, which may have been the home that he and his disciples stayed at when they were in the village.

There he found that Peter's mother-in-law was sick in bed with a fever. He healed her. And how does a Jewish mother say thank you? "She got up and prepared a meal for him" (Matthew 8:15 GWT).

By then, word had already spread throughout the village. Crowds of sick folks swarmed Peter's house. Jesus healed each one. These healing miracles, along with his dynamic and insightful preaching, made him the headliner among Jewish rabbis.

That drew the attention of top Jewish leaders in Jerusalem. Not a good thing. Crucifixion ahead.

67
Battle of the Gods on Mount Carmel

It was advantage Baal in this battle of the gods.

The object of the contest was to see which God could send down fire from the sky to light a sacrifice laid on an altar. Baal was the god of weather. He is shown in some ancient pictures holding a lightning bolt. But as the story goes, his prophets spent all morning and into the afternoon trying to convince their god to send down fire from the sky. No luck.

Elijah made fun of them and told them to pray louder. When it was Elijah's turn, he prayed a simple prayer, and the fire fell. What was Elijah's response? "'Grab the Baal prophets! Don't let one get away!' They grabbed them. Elijah had them taken down to the Brook Kishon and they massacred the lot" (1 Kings 18:40 MSG).

68
Assassination Attempt: David's Getaway

After King Saul went crazy jealous on David, envying his popularity, Saul ordered him executed. Michal (Saul's daughter and David's wife) stalled the soldiers by convincing them David was sick. "She took an idol and put it in his bed, covered it with blankets, and put a cushion of goat's hair at its head" (1 Samuel 19:13).

When they reported this to the king, he exploded. Which kinda makes sense. Why wait for a sick man to get well before you kill him?

Saul, realizing that Michal had betrayed him by helping David escape, married her off to another guy. Years later, when David became king, he ordered Michal back into his harem. Her husband wept as she left, and it doesn't sound like she was too happy either. In the harem, Michal criticized David as shameless and vulgar. The Bible's last word on her: "Michal, the daughter of Saul, remained childless throughout her entire life" (2 Samuel 6:23).

By the way, what was David doing with an idol in his house? The Bible doesn't say. Perhaps his religion in the early years was a tad eclectic. Scholars say some confused Jews seemed to worship God as the god of war while worshipping other gods for their unique specialties.

69

Sobering Up in Time for a Stroke

Nabal's name means "fool," which instantly raises questions about his parents.

Sadly, he grew into his name. His wife said so when she defended him to David, who had come to kill him. "I know Nabal is a wicked and ill-tempered man; please don't pay any attention to him. He is a fool, just as his name suggests" (1 Samuel 25:25).

What dumb thing had Nabal done? Earlier, David sent some of his men to Nabal during the festive sheep-shearing season—payday for herders. David was hoping for supplies—payback for his men helping guard Nabal's flocks. But instead of giving the men at least a little something, Nabal insulted them. "Should I take my bread and my water and my meat that I've slaughtered for my shearers and give it to a band of outlaws?" (1 Samuel 25:11).

David prepared to wipe out the entire household, but Nabal's wife intercepted the militia and stopped their attack by giving them supplies. When she got home, Nabal was sleeping off a drunk. When she told him the next morning that he nearly died, he died. Perhaps of a stroke or a heart attack.

David married the savvy widow.

70

How to Lose Your Head over a Lady

It was a husband upgrade as far as the 40-year-old Lady Herodias was concerned.

She traded in her first husband, Philip Herodias, for his brother Herod Antipas, who ruled a more prosperous region—Galilee, in what is now northern Israel.

This was incest as far as Jewish law was concerned.

- "If a man marries his brother's wife, it is an act of impurity; he has violated his brother" (Leviticus 20:21).

- "Do not have sexual relations with your brother's wife, for this would violate your brother" (Leviticus 18:16).

John the Baptist called these laws to Herod's attention. "John had been telling Herod, 'It is against God's law for you to marry your brother's wife'" (Mark 6:18). Herod's wife convinced her husband to arrest the mouthy prophet.

Later, her daughter performed an eye-popping dance for her step-daddy, Herod. He rewarded her with her choice of a gift. She consulted Mom. Mom wanted John's head.

71
The Inhospitable Herder's Wife

Hospitality was a big deal in the ancient Middle East. So it's a tad shocking to read about a herder's wife welcoming a guest and then hammering a tent peg into his head. Not very hospitable.

Hospitality was important in this land where any semblance of rest stops with food and water were few and far between. The kindness of a stranger could make the difference between life and death for a traveler.

Enemy travelers were an exception to the rule.

Sisera, the soon-to-be hammered guest, commanded a Canaanite army that had raided what is now northern Israel for 20 years. Jael and her husband weren't Jews. But grazing on Jewish lands, they sure seemed loyal to their hosts.

When Sisera arrived at their herder's camp, Jael offered him some milk—a sedative. She gave him a place to lay his weary head. Then, while he took a power nap, she staked his weary head to the ground. "Jael took a hammer and drove a tent-peg through his head into the ground, and he died" (Judges 4:21). (For more, see number 45, "Chickenhearted General.")

72

David's Elite Strike Force

Like many armies today, David's army had elite units. Two in particular. One had three men, and the other had thirty. Guess what they were called. (Don't get creative.)

- *The Three.* This unit was led by Jashobeam. "He once used his spear to kill 300 enemy warriors in a single battle" (1 Chronicles 11:11).

- *The Thirty.* This unit was led by Abishai, the brother of David's top general. Bathsheba's husband, Uriah, served in this strike force.

73

David's Trick for Conquering Jerusalem

"You'll never get in here!" That's what the defenders of Jerusalem yelled to David's army camped in the valley below, outside the walls. "Even the blind and lame could keep you out!" (2 Samuel 5:6).

What they didn't realize is that David, raised in Bethlehem, just six miles (10 km) south, knew their secret. "David had said, 'Anyone who conquers the Jebusites will have to use the water shaft'" (verse 8 TNIV). Jebusites got water from a spring outside the city walls. The spring was hidden in a small cave at the bottom of the Jerusalem ridge, below the city. Likely, they kept that cave entrance hidden.

Above the spring, inside the city walls, the residents had dug a 15-yard vertical shaft down into the cave. The shaft worked as a well with a pond-like spring resting in the cave below.

For David's strike force, the shaft worked like a ladder into the city.

74
Church-Planting Strategy: Bypass Intellectuals

Paul used a shrine in Athens—the Oxford of his day—to hook the attention of religion scholars in town. If only he could have kept their attention.

> Men of Athens, I notice that you are very religious in every way, for as I was walking along I saw your many shrines. And one of your altars had this inscription on it: "To an Unknown God." This God, whom you worship without knowing, is the one I'm telling you about (Acts 17:22-23).

Many Greeks said they believed in an afterlife. But their version involved a disembodied soul, not a reanimated corpse. So when Paul reported the story of Jesus rising from the dead, many of the Greek scholars took it as the punch line to a joke. "When they heard Paul speak about the resurrection of the dead, some laughed in contempt…That ended Paul's discussion with them" (Acts 17:32-33 msg).

Others said they wanted to hear more, and they became believers. But apparently not enough to keep Paul in town. He moved on to Corinth, about a two-day walk south (45 miles, or 72 km). He stayed there for a year and a half, starting a church that probably met in someone's home.

75

Don't Put This Guy on the Church Board

Paul ordered Christians in Corinth to kindly excommunicate a member of the church. Why?

Mother was his lover. "It is actually being said that there is sexual sin among you. And it is a kind that does not happen even among people who do not know God. A man there has his father's wife" (1 Corinthians 5:1 ncv).

Most Bible experts speculate that the woman was probably the man's stepmother. We can hope, since most would probably agree that's a tad less disgusting than a man having sex with his birth mother.

The apostle Paul simply calls her "his father's wife," perhaps because that phrasing tracks nicely with the Jewish law forbidding the relationship as incest: "Whoever has sexual intercourse with his father's wife will be cursed" (Deuteronomy 27:20 gwt).

Paul wasn't simply trying to boot the guy out of church. He was trying to rattle his cage, hoping he would come to his senses: "Then his sinful nature will be destroyed. His spirit will be saved on the day the Lord returns" (1 Corinthians 5:5 nirv).

76

There Goes the Jewish Neighborhood

The first non-Jew on record to join the Christian movement was Cornelius, a Roman from Italy (Acts 10).

Many Jews considered non-Jews as ritually unclean. That means if a Jew touched one or went into a Gentile's house, the Jew would have to go through cleaning rituals before he could worship God at the Jerusalem temple. But the book of Acts says God helped Peter change that way of thinking.

First, God gave him a vision of ritually unclean animals being lowered from heaven on a sheet. A voice told Peter to eat them. When Peter refused, saying he ate only kosher food, the voice replied, "Do not call something unclean if God has made it clean" (verse 15).

Suddenly messengers arrived calling Peter to the home of Cornelius. Along the way, Peter figured out the meaning of the vision. When he arrived at the home of Cornelius, he said so: "You know it is against our laws for a Jewish man to enter a Gentile home like this or to associate with you. But God has shown me that I should no longer think of anyone as impure or unclean" (verse 28).

77

Paul, Sounding like a Bigot

Paul evidently wasn't enamored with folks on the island of Crete. He wrote, "Cretans are always liars, evil animals, and lazy people who do nothing but eat" (Titus 1:12-13 NCV).

Paul was quoting one of Crete's own poets. In a poem called *Cretica*, Epimenides said the king of Crete told the god Zeus, "Cretans, always liars, evil beasts, idle bellies." That was about 600 years before Paul. Another Cretan poet writing about 200 years before Paul also dissed his own people. His name was Callimachus.

With that kind of self-loathing going on, the Greek word for Cretan, *Kretizo*, became a verb that means "to lie."

It's one thing for Cretans to say nasty things about themselves, many would argue. But it's quite another for someone else to pick up those words and use them—and for those words to end up in the Holy Bible.

Some Bible scholars argue that Paul was simply writing to his associate, Titus, to confirm that Titus had a hard job ahead of him. Paul had assigned him to find good men to lead churches in cities throughout the island. These scholars argue that if Paul had known that his words would end up in the Bible, forever offending Cretans, he probably would not have quoted that particular Cretan poem.

78
Jewish Tax Dodgers: Busted

Babylonian king Nebuchadnezzar wasn't just boss of the Middle East. He was a tax collector with an attitude. "During Jehoiakim's reign, King Nebuchadnezzar of Babylon invaded the land of Judah. Jehoiakim surrendered and paid him tribute for three years but then rebelled" (2 Kings 24:1).

Empires operated a bit like a neighborhood mafia boss who insists that local businesses give him a percentage of their profit in return for his protection. And if they didn't want his protection, he beat them up to prove that they needed it.

Nebuchadnezzar paid the Jews three visits, each intended to enforce his rule.

- *604 BC.* He demoted King Jehoiakim to a servant king who had to pay taxes to him.

- *597 BC.* He crushed the Jewish revolt, took the king and 10,000 others captive, and installed a new king, leaving only the poorer Jews.

- *586 BC.* He leveled Jewish cities, including Jerusalem, effectively dismantling the Jewish nation and erasing it from the world map.

79
When Iran Was Nice to Israel

Persian ruler Cyrus was surprisingly kind to the Jews. "Cyrus king of Persia says: The LORD, the God of heaven…has appointed me to build a Temple for him at Jerusalem in Judah. Now may the LORD your God be with all of you who are his people. You are free to go to Jerusalem" (2 Chronicles 36:23 CEV).

Cyrus not only freed the Jews to go home but also added this note to his declaration: "Let their neighbors contribute toward their expenses by giving them silver and gold, supplies for the journey, and livestock, as well as a voluntary offering for the Temple of God in Jerusalem" (Ezra 1:4).

This Bible story has archaeological support to back it up: a nine-inch-long (23 cm) clay cylinder called the Cylinder of Cyrus, dating from 536 BC. That coincides with Cyrus's reign, which stretched from 559 to 530 BC.

Babylonians from what is now Iraq had destroyed Jerusalem in 586 BC and deported the Jewish survivors. But 50 years later, a coalition of Medes and Persians from what is now Iran conquered the Babylonians to become the new superpower of the Middle East.

The Cylinder of Cyrus, inscribed with wedge-shaped cuneiform letters, confirms the new emperor's policy of freeing all political prisoners, not just the Jews. It says he freed all the people west of the Tigris River (in what is now Iraq) "and returned them to their homes."

80

Stephen King of the New Testament

It's not that Paul wrote horror stories like Stephen King. It's that Paul did a lot of writing like Stephen King.

The New Testament has 27 books. Thirteen claim Paul as the author.

The reason Paul wrote so much is that he traveled so much. He covered an estimated 10,000 miles (16,000 km), helping start churches mainly in modern-day Turkey and Greece.

He didn't usually stay in one place very long. So he wrote letters to congregations and their leaders, giving them advice and encouragement. Folks kept those letters, copied them, and passed them around to be read in worship services.

81

Brighter than the Desert Sun at Noon

The apostle Paul was an odd choice to lead the Christian movement. It would have been a bit like hiring Genghis Khan to head up the Peace Corps.

On the other hand, when you have to deal with a bunch of intolerant Jewish traditionalists—Christianity's first major enemies—why not hire a former intolerant Jewish traditionalist?

That's what Paul (also called Saul) was. "Saul wanted to arrest any man or woman who followed the way of Christ and imprison them in Jerusalem" (Acts 9:2 GWT).

Paul was a Pharisee—a Jewish legalist to the core. He and his fellow Pharisees were so obsessed with obeying the laws of Moses that they created extra laws to make sure they didn't break any of the main laws. Essentially, they used their laws as an army of bodyguards to shield the laws of Moses—and they expected everyone to respect their laws as much as they respected the laws of Moses.

For example, Moses said Jews shouldn't work on the Sabbath. Pharisees defined *work* to include the practice of medicine. That's why they got really ticked when Jesus healed people on the Sabbath.

Paul admitted, "I attacked the church of God and tried to destroy it…I tried harder than anyone else to follow the teachings handed down by our ancestors" (Galatians 1:13-14 NCV). But then he was converted to Christianity after a light brighter than the desert's noontime sun blinded him while he was traveling from Jerusalem to Damascus.

If you need someone to defend Christianity to a Pharisee, who better than Paul?

82

Fight or Flight: Jews on the Run

Israel's dozen tribes divided their land by lots, which may have worked a bit like flipping coins or tossing dice.

The tribe of Dan had the bad luck of getting assigned a small plug of land that, on a map, looks like a comma that starts on the seacoast around modern-day Tel Aviv and curves southward into the hills. The Philistines, a warrior race, lived in that comma.

Even Samson, who happened to be from the tribe of Dan, couldn't defeat the Philistines.

So shortly after Samson, most of the tribe packed it up and moved about 100 miles (160 km) north—beyond the Sea of Galilee. They set up their new home at the foot of the largest mountain in the region, with snow that provided the headwaters of the Jordan River—Mount Hermon, altitude 9232 feet.

> The men of Dan came to the town of Laish, whose people were peaceful and secure. They attacked with swords and burned the town to the ground...Then the people of the tribe of Dan rebuilt the town and lived there. They renamed the town Dan after their ancestor (Judges 18:27-29).

83

Philistine Secret Weapon—Not Goliath

The Iron Age came to the Philistines before it came to the Jews, who were stuck with weapons and tools made of a softer metal—bronze. "Whenever the Israelites wanted to get an iron point put on a cattle prod, they had to go to the Philistines" (1 Samuel 13:20 CEV).

Iron itself was no secret. It's one of the most abundant elements on earth. The secret was how to use billows to stoke a furnace hot enough to melt and forge the iron. Philistines discovered how to get the temperature up over 2000 degrees Fahrenheit. That's high enough to produce a low grade of wrought iron.

84

David the Music Therapist

King Saul started fighting bouts of depression after he disobeyed God and the prophet Samuel said God was no longer with Saul. Saul's advisers knew about the young shepherd boy David and his musical gift, so they recruited him to play for the king when Saul was having troubles.

David apparently worked as Saul's music therapist for several years—even before David fought his famous battle with Goliath. After David won that battle, he became Israel's instant hero, making him more famous than King Saul. That only got Saul more depressed, and it gave him a perceived enemy to target as a source of his depression. "He was sitting at home, his spear in his hand, while David was playing music. Suddenly, Saul tried to skewer David with his spear, but David ducked" (1 Samuel 19:9-10 MSG).

In time, Saul ordered his men to assassinate David. That's when David hit the trail, became a refugee, and formed a militia. When Saul died, David eventually replaced him as king of Israel.

85

Daniel Nearly Prayed Himself to Death

After serving as a royal advisor in the Iraq-based Babylonian Empire, Daniel got picked up to do more of the same for the next Middle Eastern superpower, the Iran-based Persian Empire.

Persian King Darius, who reigned from about 521 to 486 BC, appointed Daniel as one of his top three administrators. Daniel did such a great job, the king decided to promote him to number one.

The other two administrators didn't like that plan at all, so they hatched a plan of their own to get Daniel out of the way.

They knew that Daniel prayed to God every day, so playing off of the king's vanity, they said, "King Darius, during the next 30 days don't let any of your people pray to any god or man except to you. If they do, throw them into the lions' den" (Daniel 6:7 NIRV).

When the king was forced to throw his good friend Daniel to the lions, he realized the other two administrators had manipulated him. So after Daniel survived the night in the lions' den, Darius had the other administrators and their families thrown to the lions. Cat food.

86
Daniel: Dragon Killer

The unusual story of Bel and the Dragon isn't in the Protestant Bible or the Jewish Bible, but it is in many Catholic and Orthodox Christians' Bibles.

As the story goes, one of the Babylonian temples hosted a dragon, which the people revered. It was probably a snake, many scholars say. Daniel decided to kill it to prove it was just an animal and not a god. He chose a unique weapon—a hairball. "Daniel took pitch [tar], fat, and hair, and boiled them together and made cakes, which he fed to the Dragon. The dragon ate them, and burst open" (Bel and the Dragon 1:27 RSV).

The hairball cakes that Daniel fed the critter expanded once the tar, fat, and stomach juices absorbed into the hair—a bit like someone pulling the cord on an inflatable lifeboat after Jaws swallowed it.

87

When Resurrection Was a New Idea

Old Testament Jews didn't talk much about life after death.

They talked about the godly dead resting or going to be with their fathers. But they rarely mentioned resurrection and eternal life.

The idea does show up in the book of Daniel (which came late in Jewish history). Daniel didn't seem to know about the resurrection until an angelic being came to interpret his visions of the future. Daniel's story ends with the heavenly messenger saying, "So, Daniel, be faithful until the end! You will rest, and at the end of time, you will rise from death to receive your reward" (Daniel 12:13 CEV).

Based on passages like this, some Jews in Jesus's time concluded that there must be an afterlife. Pharisees taught that. Sadducees didn't. They said, "There is no resurrection from the dead" (Matthew 22:23).

88

King David's Music

In David's last words—the lyrics of a song—he calls himself "the sweet psalmist of Israel" (2 Samuel 23:1). Almost half of the Bible's psalms, 73 of the 150, are described as "a psalm of David." But that doesn't necessarily mean he wrote them.

Of is a vague word. It could mean a psalm is by David, about David, dedicated to David, or inspired by David.

But outside of the book of Psalms—a hymnbook-style collection of Jewish songs and poems—other writers reported that David was a gifted musician. He played the lyre. He organized the music ministry at the Jerusalem worship center. And he wrote songs.

When Saul and Jonathan died in battle, David wrote a funeral song with the famous lyric, "How the mighty have fallen" (2 Samuel 1:27 NKJV).

89

David Fights Outside His Weight Class

When shepherd boy David went into mortal combat with the Philistine champion Goliath, one part of Goliath's weaponry probably weighed as much as David. "His bronze coat of mail weighed 125 pounds [57 kg]" (1 Samuel 17:5).

Goliath's spear must have been heavy too. The iron spearhead alone weighed as much as a 15-pound (6.8 kg) bowling ball. That would fill an enemy's chest cavity.

David was just a boy when he walked out onto the battlefield to meet Goliath.

King Saul gave David his own armor to wear—a bronze helmet and a coat of mail. David suited up, strapped on a sword, and took a few steps.

"I can't go in these," he said.

"David took them off again. He picked up five smooth stones from a stream and put them into his shepherd's bag. Then, armed only with his shepherd's staff and sling, he started across the valley to fight the Philistine" (1 Samuel 17:39-40).

90

King Saul's Most Embarrassing Moment

Saul went crazy-jealous on David.

He resented the fact that after David killed the Philistine champion, Goliath, and followed that up with other military exploits, David had become Israel's number one hero.

Saul did not like being number two.

Ironically, he may well have been doing Number Two when David managed to sneak up behind him and clip off part of his robe.

It happened on a manhunt. Saul had all he could take of David, so he ordered him assassinated. David fled and hid in some caves at an oasis near the Dead Sea. Saul and his men followed him there. Of the many caves in the area, Saul picked the wrong one for a little privacy: "Saul went in to go to the toilet. David and his men were far back in the cave" (1 Samuel 24:2-3 NIRV).

Whatever King Saul was doing to "relieve himself," as some Bible translations politely put it, he was doing it long enough for David and his men to discuss the possibility of killing him. And long enough for David to sneak up behind him, cut off part of the robe, and then retreat to the back of the cave.

After Saul left the cave and walked a safe distance away, David yelled out to him and held up the piece of robe. He did it to prove he would never do anything to harm the king.

Humiliated on so many levels, Saul went home.

91
Advantage: Left-Handed Assassin

In the days of Samson and Gideon, an obese foreign king named Eglon oppressed the Israelites for 18 years. An Israelite named Ehud decided enough was enough. "Ehud made himself a sword with two edges, about eighteen inches [46 cm] long" (Judges 3:16 NCV).

The big bull's-eye of a target lived in what is now the Arab country of Jordan. Each year he demanded tribute from the Jews—taxes.

One year, Ehud was chosen to deliver that payment. He strapped the sword to his right hip under his clothes. Guards searching someone would typically frisk a person's left side because that's where a right-handed man would carry a sword or a knife.

When Ehud delivered the payment, he told the king that he had a message for him from God. The king cleared the room. Ehud stabbed him. "Even the handle sank in, and the blade came out his back. The king's fat covered the whole sword" (Judges 3:27 NCV).

Ehud left the weapon where it was and escaped through a room identified by a perplexing Hebrew word. Some Bible translations guess it refers to a porch. Others guess a private chamber, such as an indoor toilet.

92
Lowest Spot on Earth

The lowest dry land on the face of the earth is the shore of the Dead Sea, also known in the Bible as the Salt Sea (Genesis 14:3 NKJV). It's almost a quarter of a mile below sea level—1294 feet.

With no outlet, the Dead Sea is the drainage pit of the Middle East. It's where the Jordan River ends and nothing much begins.

Even fish can't live in this water. It's roughly 25 percent salt, making it about four times saltier than the ocean. People can't sink in this water. They float.

One tip—don't get the water in your eyes. It feels like jalapeño juice. I know.

On a personal note, I once led a three-busload group of Sunday school teachers on a visit to Israel to prep them for a series of lessons about Jesus. One lady lost her luggage. As each day went by she got more and more depressed at having to wear the same clothes.

She was really bummed out by the time we reached the Dead Sea. Her husband, a pastor, bought her a T-shirt in the gift store with a message printed on the front: "The lowest place on earth."

She wore it the rest of the day. I'm afraid I laughed out loud when I saw it. Shame on me.

We took her shopping in Jerusalem. Her luggage arrived, eventually.

93

Delilah Was a Lousy Girlfriend

Delilah turned her lover, Samson, over to his archenemies, the Philistines. She sold out her boyfriend for what may have been her weight in silver. The rulers of the five major Philistine city-kingdoms had told her, "Each one of us will give you twenty-eight pounds [12.5 kg] of silver" (Judges 16:5 NCV).

Scholars say they don't know what that much silver would have bought in her day, but it would have been enough to buy 275 slaves in the time of Joseph. His brothers sold him to slave traders for about eight ounces (228 g) (Genesis 38:28 NCV).

94

Samson's Dumb Decision

As Samson drifted off to sleep at Delilah's place, what made him think he wouldn't wake up with a buzz haircut? He had just told Delilah that if anyone cut his hair, he would "become as weak as anyone else" (Judges 16:17).

Then he took a nap—resting his head on her lap. He might as well have put it on a platter.

Samson did this after Delilah had already tried three times to weaken him.

- *Bow strings.* "Samson told [Delilah], 'If they were to tie me up with seven bowstrings...then I would become weak'...She tied him up with them" (Judges 16:7-8 MSG).

- *New ropes.* "Samson told her, 'If someone ties me up tightly with new ropes that have never been used, I will be like any other man.' So Delilah took some new ropes and tied him up" (verses 11-12 GWT).

- *Hair braids.* "Samson replied, 'Just weave the seven braids of my hair with the other threads in the loom.' So Delilah tied his braids to the loom shuttle" (verses 13-14 GWT).

Why Samson finally told this woman the truth and then fell asleep in her lap, expecting to wake up with hair, seems beyond the borders of common sense.

95
How Stoned Was Paul?

A mob in the city of Lystra, in what is now Turkey, dragged Paul outside their city and stoned him until they thought he was dead. He wasn't. In fact, "He got up and went back into the town" (Acts 14:20).

Oddly enough, just before the stoning, another mob had tried to sacrifice animals to him, mistaking him for a god.

Paul and Barnabas had arrived in town, preaching about Jesus. Paul healed a man who had been crippled since birth. It was such a dramatic miracle that folks in town concluded that Barnabas was Zeus, the chief god, and that Paul was Hermes, the chief speaker for the gods.

Lystra had a temple devoted to Zeus. When the temple priest heard about the miracle, he brought a bull to sacrifice to the men. Paul and Barnabas assured the priest and the crowd that they were not gods.

Jews arrived from previous towns where Paul and Barnabas had preached. They were militantly opposed to Paul and Barnabas's message—that Jesus was the Messiah and the Son of God. They stirred the locals into a mob that stoned Paul.

After the stoning, when the mob left, the group of believers gathered around Paul. He got up and went with them back into town. He and Barnabas moved on to the next city the following day.

96

Missionary Breakup

Missionaries Paul and Barnabas got into an argument after their first missionary trip and decided to go their separate ways. Here's what happened.

John Mark, nicknamed Mark and traditionally considered the writer of the Gospel of Mark, joined Barnabas and Paul on their first missionary trip. He traveled with them across the island of Cyprus, but as soon as they hit the coastal swampland of southern Turkey, he bailed. Mark went home.

When it came time for the second trip, "Barnabas wanted to take John Mark with them. But Paul didn't think it was wise to take him. Mark had deserted them [on the first trip]" (Acts 15:37-38 NIRV). Paul didn't want to take someone he couldn't rely on. Barnabas insisted—John Mark was his cousin.

Paul and Barnabas parted company. Barnabas went back to the island of Cyprus. Paul went to Turkey, taking a new partner named Silas.

Paul and John Mark eventually seemed to settle their differences, because the two traveled together later (see Colossians 4:10; 2 Timothy 4:11).

97

Looking for Eden

The book of Genesis gives us a clue about where the Garden of Eden was located. "A river watered the garden and then flowed out of Eden and divided into four branches…Pishon…Gihon… Tigris…Euphrates" (Genesis 2:10-14).

We know where the Tigris and Euphrates rivers are but not

the Pishon and Gihon. They may have dried up. There's evidence of ancient, now-dry riverbeds intersecting with the Tigris and Euphrates.

The Tigris and Euphrates—two of the largest rivers in the Middle East, after Egypt's Nile—start in the mountains of Turkey. They flow south through Iraq, emptying into the Persian Gulf. These two rivers put the "fertile" in "Fertile Crescent," the crescent-shaped plug of land where many say human civilization began. That's mainly in Iraq.

Students of the Bible have been searching for Eden for decades. One theory puts Eden in the mountains of Turkey. Another theory puts Eden underwater in what is now the Persian Gulf. As that theory goes, the Persian Gulf was originally a river valley before ice from the Ice Age melted, flooding the valley with ocean water.

According to that theory, the Genesis writer reversed the flow of Eden's river to hide the location of the Garden. Instead of Eden's river flowing out of the mountains and branching off into four other rivers, the four rivers merged into the Garden of Eden's river, which now lies under the Persian Gulf.

98
The Nile: A Stream in the Desert

Egypt's footprint is almost the size of Texas, Oklahoma, and Kansas combined. But most of it is barren desert. The livable land is only about the size of Maryland. This fertile land stretches only about ten miles (1.6 km) wide, snaking alongside the banks of the drought-proof Nile River.

Egyptian records confirm that when drought struck the ancient Middle East, herders migrated to the Nile River, just as the Bible says Jacob and his family did during a seven-year drought. "The total number of Jacob's direct descendants who went with him to Egypt, not counting his sons' wives, was sixty-six…As they neared their destination, Jacob sent Judah ahead to meet Joseph and get directions to the region of Goshen" (Genesis 46:26,28).

Goshen was the best grazing area in Egypt. It was in the northern delta area, where the Nile River fans out into a bunch of streams that empty into the Mediterranean Sea.

99

Season of Plagues

When the king of Egypt refused to free the Jews, Moses twisted his arm.

Ten times. Ten plagues.

It started with turning the Nile River blood red. Some students of the Bible say God may have flipped a switch, setting off a domino effect of natural disasters.

1. *Flood.* As the theory goes, the disasters started with the usual autumn flooding of the Nile River Valley. But the floodwater picked up some red algae-like toxins from swamps upriver in the heart of Africa.

2. *Frogs* flee the poisoned river.

3. *Gnats* breed in pools of receding water.

4. *Flies* lay eggs in decaying frogs and other animals killed by the tainted water.

5. *Livestock* die, possibly diseased by anthrax from the water.

6. *Boils* form on people's skin, perhaps from flies carrying the disease.

7. *Hail* is common in the area.

8. *Locusts* are also common.

9. *Darkness for three days*—a springtime sandstorm Egyptians today call "50 days."

10. *Death of oldest children.* This could be from contaminated grain. Firstborn kids sometimes got an extra helping.

Jews today mark the last plague and their release from slavery with the Passover festival, as God commanded: "Remember this day and celebrate it each year as a festival in my honor" (Exodus 12:14 CEV).

An Egyptian document, *Admonitions of Ipuwer*, reports a series of similar natural disasters, including this: "The river is blood. People refused to drink it and thirst for water." This document was written about 1300–1200 BC, which some scholars say is roughly the time of Moses. Other scholars place Moses in the 1400s BC.

100
David at Home in Goliath's Hometown

When David was on the run from King Saul, he and his militia of fugitives found a safe haven in Gath, a city in Philistia. It was the hometown of Goliath, the Philistine champion he had killed several years earlier. Saul refused to chase him into enemy territory on what is now Israel's Mediterranean coast.

The city's king, Achish, assumed David had switched sides. "Achish trusted David and thought, 'David's people must be furious with him. From now on he will have to take orders from me'" (1 Samuel 27:12 CEV).

David took his men on raids into what the Philistine king thought was Jewish territory. Instead, David was secretly wiping out Philistine communities. "David killed everyone in the towns he attacked. He thought, 'If I let any of them live, they might come to Gath and tell what I've really been doing'" (verse 11 CEV).

101
King Saul: Priest Killer

King Saul ordered the slaughter of every Jewish priest in the town of Nob—85 priests in all. "Saul shouted to his bodyguards, 'These priests of the LORD helped David! They knew he was running away, but they didn't tell me. Kill them!'" (1 Samuel 22:17 CEV).

But King Saul was wrong.

The priests did give David and his men some food, and they even gave David the sword of Goliath, which they had kept as a relic of God's protection. But they weren't helping a fugitive. They thought they were helping Saul's son-in-law and Israel's top warrior.

As one of the priests explained, "There's not an official in your administration as true to you as David, your own son-in-law and captain of your bodyguard. None more honorable either…I have no idea what you're trying to get at with this 'outlaw' talk" (1 Samuel 22:14-15 MSG).

Saul, insane with jealousy over David's popularity among the people, ordered the priests executed.

His men refused the order. Saul got the job done by a mercenary in his militia named Doeg. He was from Edom, in what is now the Arab country of Jordan.

102

Priests Who Slept with the Help

High priest Eli had two sons, both of them priests. They exploited their power, seducing women who worked at the worship center and helping themselves to whatever sacrificial meat they wanted—even meat that Jewish law said was devoted to God and should be burned on the altar.

The Bible writer describes the sons of Eli this way: "Eli's sons, Hophni and Phinehas, were good-for-nothing priests; they had no faith in the Lord" (1 Samuel 2:12 GWT).

They died in battle when Israelite soldiers asked them to bring Israel's most sacred relic to the battlefield—the Ark of the Covenant, a chest that held the Ten Commandments. It didn't go well. "The Ark of God was taken by the Philistines, and Eli's two sons, Hophni and Phinehas, died" (1 Samuel 4:11 NCV).

103

Israel's Lost Ark

After Philistines captured Israel's Ark of the Covenant, a chest that held the Ten Commandments, they took it to one of their main cities, Ashdod, as a war trophy. But "the LORD caused a lot of trouble for the [Philistine] people…He made sores break out all over their bodies" (1 Samuel 5:6 CEV).

Leaders linked the trouble to the Ark. They sent the Ark to another city—Gath. Same thing happened there. Some sort of skin sores or tumors.

They sent the Ark to Ekron. Same result.

Three strikes and the Ark was out. Philistines loaded the Ark onto an oxcart and pointed the oxen toward Israel.

Israelites had apparently lost their worship center after Philistines overran the area during an earlier battle. So the Jews put their Ark in storage at the home of a man named Abinadab. His son took care of it for 20 years until King David brought it to Jerusalem.

104
The Disappearing Army

Assyrian king Sennacherib, from what is now Iraq, surrounded Jerusalem with his army in 701 BC. Jerusalem's King Hezekiah prayed for God to save his city from the Assyrian invaders. The prophet Isaiah assured the king that God heard his prayer and would rescue Jerusalem.

When Hezekiah woke up the next morning, the Assyrians were gone. The Bible explains what had happened.

> That night the angel of the LORD went out to the Assyrian camp and killed 185,000 Assyrian soldiers. When the surviving Assyrians woke up the next morning, they found corpses everywhere. Then King Sennacherib of Assyria broke camp and returned to his own land. He went home to his capital of Nineveh and stayed there (2 Kings 19:35-36).

Back home, Sennacherib bragged about his invasion of the Jewish nation. His brag is preserved on a six-sided clay prism. His words add credibility to the Bible story because although he said he conquered 46 of their cities, he stopped short of saying he conquered Jerusalem.

Instead he said, "As for Hezekiah, I made [him] a prisoner in Jerusalem, his royal residence, like a bird in a cage. I surrounded him."

A Greek historian named Herodotus, who wrote about 250 years later, added more to the story. He said Sennacherib was headed to Egypt but was stopped one night by an infestation of mice. He said the mice ate bowstrings, leather shields, and other equipment. Somehow, they also killed many soldiers.

Some scholars suggest the mice may have carried the bubonic plague.

105

Samuel's Mom Gave Him Away

Heartbroken about not being able to have any children, Hannah took her prayer to Israel's tent worship center. The Israelites had pitched their sacred tent in the hills of Shiloh—about ten miles (16 km) north of Hannah's home in Ramah. Hannah and her husband went there every year to worship.

Weeping, Hannah prayed, "Please give me a son! If you do, I'll give him back to you. Then he will serve you all the days of his life" (1 Samuel 1:11 NIRV). She would give the boy back to God, and he would serve at the worship center.

God answered her prayer, so Hannah kept her end of the deal. "When the boy didn't need her to nurse him anymore, she took him with her to Shiloh" (verse 24 NIRV).

Little Samuel's parents visited him, but the priest Eli raised him. "Each year his mother made him a little robe. She took it to him when she went up to Shiloh with her husband. She did it when her husband went to offer the yearly sacrifice" (1 Samuel 2:19 NIRV).

Eli blessed Hannah, asking that God would give her more children. God did—"three sons and two daughters" (verse 21).

106

Veggies: Bad for One Jew's Health

Israel's King Ahab had a getaway palace in the city of Jezreel. He told his neighbor, Naboth, "Since your vineyard is so convenient to my palace, I would like to buy it to use as a vegetable garden" (1 Kings 21:2).

Naboth refused because the land had been in his family for many generations. And he wanted to give that land to his children. Ahab, a Jew himself, understood Naboth's feelings, but he became depressed because he really wanted that veggie garden.

Ahab's wife, Jezebel, wasn't particularly famous for her Hebrew sensitivities. She was not an Israelite. She came from what is now the country of Lebanon. She arranged for some men to make false accusations against Naboth, who ended up getting stoned to death. Jezebel confiscated his land for her husband.

107

Weather Forecast: Drought

The prophet Elijah declared a drought on Israel, challenging a god who specialized in producing rain—a god famous in ancient times as lord of fertility in fields, flocks, and families. Statues and pictures of Baal sometimes show him holding what appears to be thunderbolts.

Oddly enough, some Jews seem to have worshipped both Baal and God. Some scholars speculate that those Jews considered God the go-to god of war. But when it came to needing rain or making babies, they followed the lead of their Canaanite neighbors by offering sacrifices to Baal.

Elijah challenged the prophets of Baal to a contest. He arranged to have a bull sacrificed and placed on an altar and said, "You pray to your god. And I'll pray to the LORD. The god who answers by sending fire down is the one and only God" (1 Kings 18:24 NIRV). The Jews would worship the first god to burn up the sacrifice by sending fire from the sky—perhaps lightning.

Oddsmakers would probably have favored Baal, the god of rain and lightning.

Elijah bet on the Lord, God of everything. It was a good bet. (See "Battle of the Gods on Mount Carmel," number 67.)

108
Vacuumed into Heaven

When it came time for the prophet Elijah to leave the planet, he left in style. "Elijah and Elisha were walking along and talking, when suddenly there appeared between them a flaming chariot pulled by fiery horses. Right away, a strong wind took Elijah up into heaven" (2 Kings 2:11 CEV).

Folks looking for a natural explanation of what happened might see in this story some lightning ("flaming chariot") and a tornado ("strong wind"). Tornados are rare in the area of Israel and Jordan, but they do show up from time to time. Most students of the Bible prefer a more literal read of the story, which implies a supernatural event. In either case, storm clouds and lightning do show up elsewhere in the Bible, representing God's arrival.

- *Ezekiel's vision of God.* "I saw a storm coming from the north. There was an immense cloud with flashing lightning surrounded by a bright light" (Ezekiel 1:4 GWT).

- *God's appearance at Mount Sinai.* "Thunder roared and

lightning flashed, and a dense cloud came down on the mountain…The LORD came down on the top of Mount Sinai" (Exodus 19:16,20).

109

God's Cure for Depression

Elijah defeated 850 pagan prophets in a contest to see whose god could send down fire from the sky to burn up an altar. Elijah then ordered the crowd to execute the false prophets.

Yet when he got word that Queen Jezebel put a hit out on him, he ran south toward Israel's badlands—not stopping until he reached Beersheba, a village some 100 miles (160 km) away.

Once there, thoroughly depressed, he asked God to kill him.

God had a better idea. "An angel touched him and told him, 'Get up and eat!'" (1 Kings 19:5). Elijah enjoyed a meal of hot bread and water, followed by a good sleep, followed by another meal.

110

How to Stop a River

Joshua and the Israelites needed to cross the Jordan River during springtime flooding. What to do?

"As soon as the feet of the priests who were carrying the Ark touched the water at the river's edge, the water above that point began backing up a great distance away at a town called Adam" (Joshua 3:15-16).

The Ark of the Covenant was Israel's most sacred relic. It was a gold-covered chest that held the Ten Commandments. The writer telling Joshua's story implies that God used the Ark to perform a miracle, much as God had earlier used Moses's staff to part the Red Sea for the Jewish refugees fleeing Egypt.

Some students of the Bible say they wonder if this was more a miracle of timing.

The Jordan River runs along a fault line. Several earthquakes have dropped landslides of cliffs into the Jordan River, damming it up. Two occurred in 1906 and 1956, but the most remarkable landslide took place in 1927. Cliffs 150 feet (46 m) high near the ruins of Adam—which many scholars say is the very site mentioned in the Bible—tumbled into the Jordan River and dammed it up for 21 hours.

The site is about 20 miles (32 km) upriver from Jericho.

111
Free Health Care

Elisha cured a Syrian military officer's skin disease and then politely refused the man's gift, which amounted to millions of dollars. He said, "As surely as the LORD lives, whom I serve, I will not accept any gifts" (2 Kings 5:16).

Most Bible translations call the disease leprosy, but the original Hebrew word could mean any number of skin diseases.

Elisha told the man, Naaman, to wash himself in the muddy Jordan River seven times. Naaman balked at first but did it anyhow.

Good thing. It worked.

As a thank-you gift, Naaman had brought…

- 10 sets of fine clothing
- 750 pounds (340 kg) of silver, worth more than $200,000 today

- 150 pounds (68 kg) of gold, worth almost $3 million today

After Elisha refused the gifts, his servant tried to sneak some by telling Naaman that his master had agreed to accept two sets of clothes and 150 pounds (68 kg) of silver after all. Elisha found out and gave his servant another gift—Naaman's skin disease.

112

The King Who Talked with the Dead

Camped with his militia on the hills of Mount Gilboa, King Saul looked down into the sprawling Jezreel Valley below.

"Saul took one look at the Philistine army and started shaking with fear. So he asked the LORD what to do. But the LORD would not answer, either in a dream or by a priest or a prophet" (1 Samuel 28:5-6 CEV).

That's when Saul resorted to finding a medium who could call up the spirit of Samuel, the prophet who had guided him during the early years of his reign. "Saul told his officers, 'Find me a woman who conjures up the dead. Then I'll go to her and ask for her services'" (1 Samuel 28:7 GWT).

Bad news from Samuel: "Tomorrow the LORD will let the Philistines defeat Israel's army, then you and your sons will join me down here in the world of the dead" (1 Samuel 28:19 CEV).

So it was.

113

The Man Who Didn't Die

Born seven generations after Adam, Enoch mysteriously disappeared.

It's easy to understand how someone could disappear. If we brainstormed a list of ways to make a person go away, we might include...

- Lion attack.

- Falling off a cliff.

- Wandering away with dementia and dying of exposure.

One brainstorm that probably wouldn't make the list is getting swooped up into heaven. The Genesis writer simply said, "One day he disappeared, because God took him" (Genesis 5:22). No explanation of how he knew this or how it happened.

Many Jews seemed to believe that everything that happened, good or bad, was God's will, so perhaps even a lion attack would have qualified as God taking Enoch. But that's not how most Jews understood the story.

More than a thousand years after Moses—traditionally considered the author of Genesis—one Jew put it this way: "It was by faith that Enoch was taken up to heaven without dying—'he disappeared, because God took him'" (Hebrews 11:5).

No lion. No cliff. No dementia.

From earth to heaven.

114
Greatest Wonder of the Ancient World

Paul started a church in Ephesus, a major city on the west coast of what is now Turkey and home to one of the Seven Wonders of the World. "Everyone knows that Ephesus is the official guardian of the temple of the great Artemis" (Acts 19:35).

Paul said Artemis was no goddess at all.

One Roman writer in the 200s BC declared the Temple of Artemis the most wonderful of all the Seven Wonders of the World. It was a massive temple by ancient standards—four times larger than the Parthenon of Athens. It stretched 130 yards (119 m) long, 70 yards (64 m) wide, and six stories high. This writer, identifying himself as Philon of Byzantium, said this about the ancient Wonders: "I have seen…

- all the walls and hanging gardens of ancient Babylon,
- the statue of Olympian Zeus,
- the Colossus of Rhodes,
- the mighty work of the high pyramids,
- and the tomb of Mausolus.

But when I saw the temple at Ephesus rising to the clouds, all these other wonders were put in the shade."

The Wonder he skipped, forgot to mention, or never saw was the Lighthouse at Alexandria, on the coast of Egypt.

115

Kicking Paul out of Town

When Paul converted so many people in Ephesus to Christianity that it threatened the idol-selling business, local merchants started a riot. They didn't want him killing the town's most famous industry—making silver idols of the city's patron goddess, Artemis. Paul called the figurines handmade gods that weren't gods at all.

The owner of the business, Demetrius, employed lots of artisans and salespeople. He rallied them and provoked a riot by saying, "Friends, you know that we make a good living at this. But you have surely seen and heard how this man Paul...claims that the gods we humans make are not really gods at all" (Acts 19:24-26 CEV). He was careful to add a religious spin: "I'm not just talking about the loss of public respect for our business. I'm also concerned that the temple of the great goddess Artemis will lose its influence" (verse 27).

The riot drove Paul out of town, though local converts kept the church alive. Paul later assigned his friend Timothy to pastor the church.

Archaeologists found Demetrius's name on a list of men honored for protecting the temple. They also found an inscription about the business: "May the guild of the silversmiths prosper."

116
Call Him Red, Not Harry

Isaac and Rebekah named their oldest son Esau, which means hairy. But he later earned the nickname Edom, which means red. It was not a compliment.

"One day, Jacob was cooking some stew, when Esau came home hungry and said, 'I'm starving to death! Give me some of that red stew right now!' That's how Esau got the name 'Edom'" (Genesis 25:29-30 CEV).

The headline in this story isn't the stew. It's the price Esau paid for it: his birthright.

As the oldest son, Esau would have inherited a double share of the family estate—twice as much as Jacob. He also would have become the leader of his extended family, which would have included Jacob's family.

The story leaves some readers thinking of Esau as dumber than a bag of peas and of Jacob as an exploitive, price-gouging jerk of a brother (and probably a good cook).

117
How Iran Got a Jewish Queen

When Persian Queen Vashti publically dissed her husband, King Xerxes, at one of his huge parties, he decided it was time for a new queen.

The question was where to find one.

The answer: a beauty contest.

That's the idea the king's advisors dreamed up—an empire-wide beauty contest to find the king a wife with some wow. "Let us search the empire to find beautiful young virgins for the king...

After that, the young woman who most pleases the king will be made queen instead of Vashti" (Esther 2:2,4).

Xerxes loved the idea.

Beauty hunters rounded up the contestants, including Esther, and took them all to the royal harem, where they got prepped to spend some quality time with the king. The eunuch in charge of the harem favored Esther and gave her advice on how to please the king.

Must have been good advice—"She pleased him more than any of the other virgins" (Esther 2:17 NIRV).

118
The Disappearing Preacher

An African official—a man from what is now southern Egypt and Sudan (then Ethiopia)—was on his way home after making a pilgrimage to Jerusalem.

The Bible says an angel told Philip to start walking on the road headed southwest out of Jerusalem toward the city of Gaza and the Mediterranean coastal road to Egypt.

There, Philip came across the official reading the book of Isaiah—chapter 53. That's the Suffering Servant passage about a mysterious man who would be beaten and executed for the sins of others.

Philip told the man about Jesus. The official was so excited that when they came across a watering place, he asked Philip to baptize him. "When they came up out of the water, the Spirit of the Lord suddenly took Philip away" (Acts 8:39 NIRV).

119

The First Jew Was an Iraqi

Remember hearing sermons or reading about God calling Abraham out of Ur of the Chaldees to go to the Promised Land?

Not quite right.

Actually, it was Abraham's dad, Terah, who decided to leave Ur (in modern-day Iraq) and move to the land of Canaan (Genesis 11:31). The Bible doesn't say why.

Tarah got two-thirds of the way there. He apparently liked the pastures in Haran, a city on what is now Turkey's border with Syria. So he settled there.

It was only after Terah died that God told Abraham, "Leave your native country, your relatives, and your father's family, and go to the land that I will show you. I will make you into a great nation...All the families on earth will be blessed through you" (Genesis 12:1-3).

That's a prophecy many scholars say continues to be fulfilled through Jesus, a Jew who descended from an Iraqi.

120

Eve Wasn't Her Name at First

"Wow" was pretty much what Adam said when he first saw his wife, who was wearing nothing but a smile. One Bible version translates his first words, "At last!" (Genesis 2:23).

The tone almost feels like "Hallelujah!"

Then Adam names her. "She will be called 'woman' [Hebrew: *ishshah*], because she was taken from 'man' [Hebrew: *ish*]."

After God told the couple that the woman would give birth to children, Adam gave his lady a new name. "Then the man—Adam—named his wife Eve, because she would be the mother of all who live" (Genesis 3:20). *Eve* sounds like a Hebrew word that means "to give life."

121

A Snake in Paradise

Was the serpent that tricked Eve into eating the forbidden fruit Satan himself? The writer of Revelation, the last book in the Bible, says yes. "That snake, who fools everyone on earth, is known as the devil and Satan" (Revelation 12:9 CEV).

But the Genesis writer doesn't identify the sneaky snake. "The snake was sneakier than any of the other wild animals that the LORD God had made. One day it came to the woman and asked, 'Did God tell you not to eat fruit from any tree in the garden?'" (Genesis 3:1 CEV).

The Jews took a long time to discover Satan, many scholars of the Bible say. It wasn't until New Testament times that Jews seemed to figure out that Satan was personal—a real entity. The story of Satan tempting Jesus offers a good picture of that.

In Old Testament times—even in the story of Job, when Satan made a deal with God to test Job—the word translated *Satan* simply means "accuser."

Between the time Genesis was written and the time Revelation was written—a span of perhaps more than a thousand years—Jews linked the serpent in the creation story to Satan.

122

Them Dry Bones

When Babylonian invaders from what is now Iraq conquered the Jewish nation and deported the survivors, God's chosen people suddenly felt unchosen.

They may have figured they broke their contract with God, which called for them to obey him in return for his blessing. As a result, they may have feared, they were doomed to suffer the consequences for the rest of history. The exiles were complaining among themselves, "We have become old, dry bones—all hope is gone. Our nation is finished" (Ezekiel 37:11).

Not quite.

God gave the prophet Ezekiel a vision of a valley of dry bones coming back to life—a picture of deported Jews returning to their homeland and rebuilding Israel. He told Ezekiel to give the exiles this assurance: "O my people, I will open your graves of exile and cause you to rise again. Then I will bring you back to the land of Israel…I will put my Spirit in you, and you will live again and return home to your own land" (Ezekiel 37:12,14).

123

A Prophet's Shave and a Trim

The prophet Ezekiel shaved his head and beard and divided the hair into three piles. He burned one pile, chopped another pile with his sword, and tossed the third pile to the wind. "This is an illustration of what will happen to Jerusalem," he said (Ezekiel 5:5).

Ezekiel predicted that invaders would lay siege to Jerusalem. Babylonians, based in present-day Iraq, did just that. They destroyed Jerusalem in 586 BC.

Here's what Ezekiel said the three piles of hair represented:

- *Burned hair.* "A third of your people will die in the city from disease and famine."
- *Chopped hair.* "A third of them will be slaughtered by the enemy outside the city walls."
- *Scattered hair.* "I [God] will scatter a third to the winds" (Ezekiel 5:12).

124
Don't Cry, the Wife Is Dead

When Ezekiel's wife died, God told him not to cry.

Ezekiel was a prophet exiled in what is now Iraq. He prophesied to fellow Jews in exile. He said that because of the sins of the Jews, God was going to allow the Jewish capital, Jerusalem, to be destroyed—along with the world's only Jewish temple.

He also said that when they got the news that Jerusalem had fallen, they would react much the same way he did to the news that his wife had died. "You won't cry or mourn, but all day long you will go around groaning because of your sins" (Ezekiel 24:23 CEV).

Bible experts don't seem able to answer the "why" question. Why would the Jews not go through their normal mourning rituals once they heard about the fall of Jerusalem?

Perhaps the news would be so devastating that it would leave them numb. Or perhaps after the temple was gone and before synagogues emerged, the Jews in Babylon couldn't practice their group rites and were reduced to suffering in isolation.

125

Divorce Your Non-Jewish Wives

This order by a priest named Ezra is going to sound harsh. But some scholars say there's no indication God approved Ezra's message.

Ezra ordered all Jewish men married to non-Jews to divorce their wives and send them away—with their kids.

Why? Jewish law forbids Jews to marry non-Jews. "Do not let your daughters and sons marry their sons and daughters, for they will lead your children away from me to worship other gods" (Deuteronomy 7:3-4).

Sure enough, when the Jews entered Canaan, they mixed with the people and started worshipping their idols. In time, the Bible says God punished the Jews by allowing invaders to level Jewish cities—Jerusalem included—and to deport the surviving Jews.

Ezra was one of many descendants of the Jewish survivors eventually allowed to return to Israel and rebuild their nation. Some Bible scholars say the ancient Jewish law—almost 1000 years old by the time of Ezra—was intended only for the Exodus Jews. These commentators suggest that Ezra and other Jews of his time seemed afraid that intermarriage would result in more punishment from God. So Ezra issued the seemingly harsh and racist order: "Divorce your foreign wives" (Ezra 10:11 CEV).

In fact, some of these scholars argue that the book of Ruth was included in the Jewish Bible as a counterpoint to Ezra. Ruth, a non-Jew from what is now the Arab country of Jordan, became the great-grandmother of David—founder of Israel's greatest dynasty of kings. (See number 53, "Arab Mother of the Jews.")

126
Paul Shipwrecked in a Typhoon

Paul was fed up.

After being held in prison at Israel's coastal city of Caesarea for two years without a trial, the apostle Paul was fed up. He appealed to the emperor's supreme court to settle his case. He had that right as a Roman citizen.

Unfortunately, it was the beginning of autumn—the risky sailing season.

Paul and his military escort made it as far as the island of Crete, about halfway to Rome. Paul, a seasoned traveler, advised wintering at the harbor of Fair Havens because "sailing was no longer safe" (Acts 27:9 CEV). But the captain wanted to go west to Phoenix, a more protected harbor on the island.

They never made it.

What sounds like a typhoon snatched the ship and drove it southwest toward the dangerously shallow water off the North African coast. Then the winds shifted and throttled the ship northwest, running it aground off the island of Malta, south of Sicily and Italy.

Fortunately, everyone survived, but the ship was destroyed.

When the dangerous sailing season ended in the spring, Paul and his military escort caught another ship headed to Italy.

127

Governor on the Take

A Roman governor kept Paul in prison for two years, hoping to squeeze bribe money out of him.

Roman soldiers arrested Paul in Jerusalem after his presence at the temple sparked a riot among the Jews. Roman officers intervened to rescue him. They took Paul to the coastal city of Caesarea, where he was held in prison.

Paul remained there for two years until a new governor named Festus replaced Felix. "Felix often sent for Paul and talked with him, because he hoped that Paul would offer him a bribe" (Acts 24:26 CEV).

Roman officials ordered Felix to Rome and charged him with abusing his authority. One of his alleged crimes was arranging the murder of a high priest who criticized him. Felix could have been executed for that and probably would have been if his brother had not appealed to Emperor Nero for mercy.

128

Paul: The End

Paul's story ends with a cliffhanger—Paul is awaiting trial in the emperor's court

"We arrived in Rome, and Paul was allowed to live in a house by himself with a soldier to guard him" (Acts 24:16 CEV). The writer never bothers to tell us what happened. We're left waiting for the trial and the verdict.

Paul had spent two years in a Judean prison in the coastal city of Caesarea after his presence in the Jerusalem temple sparked a riot among the Jews. He eventually appealed to the emperor's high court to settle his case. So the Roman governor shipped him off to Rome. As the writer in Acts reports, "For two years Paul stayed in a rented house and welcomed everyone who came to see him" (verse 30 CEV).

None of the Bible writers tell us how Paul died. Perhaps that's because everyone reading Paul's story in the first Christian century would have known.

Some Bible experts speculate that the emperor executed him after that trial in about AD 62. But a Rome-based bishop named Clement, writing about 30 years after Paul, said Paul "went to the limit of the West." Spain was the western limit of the Roman Empire. If that's where Paul went, it could mean that he survived the trial reported in Acts only to get executed during Emperor Nero's persecution of Christians in AD 64.

129
The 500-Year-Old Angel

Gabriel may have been on the job throughout Bible times, identified only as "the angel of the LORD"—a title that some scholars say could have referred to any number of angels and at times to God himself.

But Gabriel is identified by name for the first time some 500 years before Jesus in what is now Iran. As the Bible tells it, God sent Gabriel as an angelic tutor to explain a vision to the prophet Daniel. "As I, Daniel, was trying to understand the meaning of this vision…Gabriel approached the place where I was standing" (Daniel 8:15,17).

At the time, Jerusalem lay in ruins, destroyed by Babylonian invaders from what is now Iraq. But Gabriel assured Daniel that the time was coming when Jerusalem would be rebuilt and "the Anointed King will come" (Daniel 9:25 NIRV).

Five centuries later, Gabriel announced the birth of the advance man for the Anointed King, the Messiah. That advance man was John the Baptist. "He will prepare the way for the Lord" (Luke 1:17 NIRV).

In his last known appearance, Gabriel announced the birth of the Messiah himself. The angel appeared to Mary and told her she would give birth to a baby. "You must name him Jesus. He will be great and will be called the Son of the Most High God" (Luke 1:31-32 NIRV).

130

Farmer Jesus?

Jesus's hometown of Nazareth was one of 204 villages in the lush farming region of Galilee, according to Josephus, a Jewish historian from the first-century.

People in Galilee certainly worked a variety of jobs. Joseph, father of Jesus, was in the construction business as a builder. Many were herders. But according to Josephus, most people made their living by growing crops, such as grapes, olives, and barley.

As Josephus put it, "Every inch of the soil has been cultivated by the locals. The land everywhere has such rich soil producing wonderful grazing, and such a wide variety of trees, that even the laziest people are tempted to take up a career in farming."

Though Jesus's dad was a builder, farm life is the setting for many of Jesus's parables. "Jesus used stories to teach them many things. He said: 'A farmer went out to plant his seed'" (Matthew 13:3 NCV).

131
Odd Advice from the Top Jewish Scholar

The apostle Paul said he studied under the top Jewish scholar of his day—Gamaliel, a man who served on the Jewish governing council in Jerusalem. Surprisingly, when Jesus's disciples refused the council's order to stop preaching, Gamaliel said, "My advice is, leave these men alone" (Acts 5:38).

That helps explain why the Bible writer described him as "an expert in religious law and respected by all the people" (verse 34). It also helps explain why Paul name-dropped him by bragging, "I was brought up and educated here in Jerusalem under Gamaliel" (Acts 22:3).

Gamaliel was savvy. He knew that arresting the miracle-working disciples and perhaps killing them could provoke a riot, turn them into martyrs, and give a big boost to the fledgling Christian movement. So he offered this advice: "If what they are planning is something of their own doing, it will fail. But if God is behind it, you cannot stop it anyway" (Acts 5:38-39 cev).

132
Like Father, Like Son: Liar

Abraham and Isaac both feared that regional rulers would kill them and marry the gorgeous widows. So they told the same lie: "Abram said to his wife Sarai, 'I know that you're a beautiful woman. When the Egyptians see you, they'll say, "This is his wife!" Then they'll kill me but let you live. Please say that you're my sister'" (Genesis 12:11-13 gwt).

That was quite the compliment for Abraham's wife, Sarah, who was about 65 years old when Abraham told that lie in Egypt. He told the same lie in what is now Israel to King Abimelech (Genesis 20).

It was actually only half a lie. Sarah was not only his wife but also his half sister. They had the same father but different mothers. But when Abraham's son Isaac told the same lie many years later—again to King Abimelech—it was a full-fledged lie. His wife, Rebekah, was his cousin. But he told the king, "She is my sister" (Genesis 26:7).

The stories about King Abimelech are so similar that some scholars speculate that the writer or his source confused Isaac with Abraham. Others insist the history is accurate.

133
An Angel's One-Liner?

If ever an angel made a wisecrack in the Bible, this is that wisecracking angel.

Out of nowhere the angel showed up and said, "Mighty hero, the LORD is with you!" (Judges 6:12). At the time, Gideon was hiding in a hole in the ground: "Gideon was nearby, threshing grain in a shallow pit, where he could not be seen by the Midianites" (verse 11 CEV).

Maybe it wasn't a joke. Maybe the angel was being stoic and, like Spock, the Vulcan of Star Trek fame, was merely stating the facts.

- God was with Gideon.
- Gideon was destined to become famous as one of Israel's mighty heroes.

For seven years, raiders had pillaged Israel during harvest season. The raiders came from Midian, which is now in western Saudi Arabia. They stole all the crops and livestock they could find.

God chose Gideon to lead a militia to drive out the raiders. A night attack on their camp did the job.

134

Camels on the Warpath

History's first known report of camels in war shows up in the Bible's story of Gideon fighting Midianite invaders storming in from the Arabian Desert in the 1100s BC. "They came like huge numbers of locusts. It was impossible to count all of those men and their camels. They came into the land to destroy it" (Judges 6:5 NIRV).

Camels gave the raiders a huge advantage—the element of surprise. Camels could sprint up to 40 mph (64 kph), charging into a village without warning.

"The LORD turned to Gideon and said, 'Go with your strength and save Israel from the Midianites'" (Judges 6:14 NCV).

Gideon's tactic was to turn the element of surprise back on them. Though they reportedly numbered in the thousands, Gideon was able to rout them with a militia of only 300 men, equipped with an odd trio of weaponry: a torch, a clay jar to cover the torch, and a ram's horn.

Gideon's militia surrounded the invader camp at night. The men lit their torches but kept them hidden inside the clay jars. On Gideon's signal, men broke the clay jars to suddenly expose the light. Then they screamed and blew their horns.

Confused in the pitch black of night, raiders turned on one another. Survivors ran for home.

135

Fallen Hero

After Gideon and his 300-man militia routed an invasion force of Midianites, the Jewish people offered to make Gideon their king.

He refused. Instead, he asked for just one thing—that each of his soldiers give him one of the earrings they took from dead enemy soldiers.

They agreed. Gideon ended up with about 43 pounds (20 kg) of gold.

Tragically, "Gideon used the gold to make an idol and placed it in his hometown" (Judges 8:27 GWT). It may have been a vest like ones worn by kings and priests.

Maybe he intended it as a memorial to their battlefield victory. But in time, the object became sacred to the people and even to Gideon. "Soon all the Israelites prostituted themselves by worshiping it, and it became a trap for Gideon and his family" (verse 27).

136

God Is Not the Great Yahoo

When Moses asked God what God's name was, God answered, "When you go to the people of Israel, tell them, 'I AM sent me to you'" (Exodus 3:14 NCV).

Bible experts can't be sure how God pronounced his name. Jews who wrote the Old Testament used only consonants, no vowels. So the name of God shows up in the Bible as YHWH.

Scholars have to guess how to fill in the vowels. It's an important guess because this name shows up nearly 7000 times in the Bible. Many Bibles translate the name as "the LORD."

The most popular guess for how to spell God's name is YAH-WEH. For crossword aficionados who might suggest the phonetic twin of Yahoo—YAHWHO—not a chance.

Dr. Joseph Colson, a prof at Nazarene Theological Seminary and an expert in the ancient Hebrew language, put it this way: "While it could be fun, no Semitic language ever would allow all three root letters (here the HWH) to occur in succession together, in any form of any root, without vowels to break them up."

137
One God or Three?

If you see a seminar offering to explain the Trinity, some scholars would suggest skipping it.

Waste of time. They insist that no one on this planet understands the Trinity. The brightest minds in early Christian history gave up trying to figure it out. Instead, they simply decided to believe it because they saw the idea clearly taught in the Bible.

The puzzle starts with the most important Jewish belief: "The LORD is the one and only God" (Deuteronomy 6:4 NIRV). Yet Jesus said, "The Father and I are one" (John 10:30). Jesus also referred to the Holy Spirit: "You will receive power when the Holy Spirit comes upon you" (Acts 1:8).

The Bible never uses the word *Trinity*. But Jesus instructed his disciples, "Go and make followers of all people in the world. Baptize them in the name of the Father and the Son and the Holy Spirit" (Matthew 28:19 NCV).

One plus one plus one equals one? Two early Christian scholars summed up their beliefs this way:

- *One God.* "The Father is God, the Son is God, the

Holy Spirit is God…Yet we do not say that there are three gods but one God, the most exalted Trinity" (Augustine, about AD 354–430).

- *Faith trumps understanding.* "We don't understand the mystery of how this can be, or what causes it. But we trust the evidence of this truth" (Ambrose, about AD 340–397).

138

Skull Hill

Jesus died at a place that translates into English as Skull Hill. "Carrying the cross by himself, he went to the place called Place of the Skull (in Hebrew, *Golgotha*)" (John 19:17). It's *Calvary* in Latin, the language of the Romans. That word means "the skull."

Why people called the execution site Skull Place is anyone's guess. One educated guess is that it got its name from a nearby cemetery—a garden area reclaimed from an abandoned rock quarry. Or maybe the name came from the fact that people were executed at the site.

One longshot guess is that the execution site rested on top of the hill above a cliff with its face, at least in modern times, eroded to resemble a skull. It has what look like two eye sockets and the bridge of a nose. A British general named Charles Gordon (1833–1885) pitched that idea, which is now called Gordon's Calvary.

Most scholars say the actual site of Jesus's execution is preserved inside the Church of the Holy Sepulchre in Jerusalem.

139

Where to Get a Fair Trial

Without police to enforce laws, Old Testament Jews enforced the laws themselves. Often without a trial.

If one person killed another person, it was up to the victim's surviving family members to put the murderer down.

Jews who killed someone accidentally could flee to one of six "cities of refuge" scattered throughout Israel, where they could get a fair trial. If found innocent, the defendant could stay in the city—a safe haven from vengeful relatives. But if the innocent defendant left the city, protection under the law could no longer be guaranteed. Only when the high priest died could the defendant safely return home.

Bible experts guess that the rationale for this odd law is that the death of the high priest atoned for the accidental death of the victim. Blood for blood.

If, however, the defendant was found guilty of murder, Jewish law stipulated, "The victim's nearest relative is responsible for putting the murderer to death" (Numbers 35:19).

140

Don't Look to Hosea for Kid Names

God asked the prophet Hosea more than even God had a right to ask, according to some ancient Jewish scholars. They argue that the story of Hosea was either a parable or Hosea's report of a vivid dream.

For one, these scholars said they had trouble believing that a holy God would ask a prophet to marry a loosey-goosey woman. "Go. Get married to a woman who will commit adultery. Take as your own the children who will be born as a result of her adultery" (Hosea 1:2 NIRV).

Yet most scholars seem to reach the conclusion that Hosea was a real man who married a woman who would produce a dysfunctional family.

In a sense, Hosea's story *was* a parable—a living parable. His wife represented the spiritual unfaithfulness of Israel. And each of his children represented what would come of Israel's unfaithfulness.

- *Jezreel.* "Name him Jezreel. That is because I will soon punish Jehu's royal family. He killed many people at the city of Jezreel. So I will put an end to the kingdom of Israel" (verse 4 NIRV).

- *Lo-ruhamah* (Hebrew for "not loved"). "Name her Lo-Ruhamah. That is because I will no longer show love to the people of Israel. I will not forgive them anymore" (verse 6 NIRV).

- *Lo-ammi* ("not mine"). "Name him Lo-Ammi. That is because Israel is no longer my people. And I am no longer their God" (verse 9 NIRV).

141
Sodom: Barbecued

"The LORD rained down fire and burning sulfur from the sky on Sodom and Gomorrah" (Genesis 19:24).

Actually, one theory says the fire and sulfur started in the ground and worked itself up into a whopper of an explosion. As the theory goes, Sodom and Gomorrah and other cities of the plain were situated in or near what is now the southern shallows of the Dead Sea. This is a mineral-rich area that the Israelis still mine. Lots of natural gas, salt, and highly flammable sulfur.

According to the theory, a tremor in this earthquake-prone region ripped open a pocket of gas, which was ignited by a fire or a lamp in the city. Fire and minerals exploded into the sky and rained down on the plain. Some speculate that the spray of minerals is what covered Lot's wife.

142

When Guests Become Slaves

Jews weren't the only ones going to the Nile River in Egypt to weather out a drought. Ancient Egyptian records confirm that foreign shepherds from throughout the region went to the drought-proof Nile River Valley in times of famine.

That's pretty much what the Bible says Jacob did. When he was in Canaan, Joseph had sent him a message from Egypt saying, "Come here as quickly as you can. You will live near me in the region of Goshen…I will take care of you there during the next five years of famine. But if you don't come, you and your family and your animals will starve to death" (Genesis 45:9-11 CEV).

Years earlier, Joseph's brothers had sold him to slave traders who took him to Egypt. But in Egypt, Joseph rose to great authority because he was able to interpret dreams and predict the future. He had predicted a seven-year drought, so the king put him in charge of preparing for it by managing the country's grain harvest.

Joseph got the king's approval to allow his family to weather out the drought in the fertile region called Goshen. That's where the Nile River fans out into several streams that empty into the Mediterranean Sea.

The Jews overstayed their welcome. They remained in Egypt 430 years (Exodus 12:40).

Eventually, an Egyptian king became concerned. "'The people of Israel now outnumber us and are stronger than we are. We must make a plan'...So the Egyptians made the Israelites their slaves" (Exodus 1:9-11).

143

Abraham Abandons Wife and Son

Infertile Sarah told her husband, Abraham, to make a baby with their slave girl Hagar. They named the baby Ishmael.

About 14 years later, Sarah was able to have a baby after all. They named him Isaac.

According to the Middle Eastern custom of the day, the oldest son got a double share of the inheritance. So when Abraham died, his herds and all of his estate would have been divided three ways, with Ishmael getting twice as much as Isaac.

But Sarah wanted her only son, Isaac, to get everything. "Sarah said to Abraham, 'Throw out this slave woman and her son. Her son should not inherit anything; my son Isaac should receive it all'" (Genesis 21:10 NCV).

Abraham hated the idea of sending Ishmael and his mother away, but God told him it was okay. "Isaac is the son through whom your descendants will be counted. But I will also make a nation of the descendants of Hagar's son because he is your son, too" (verses 12-13).

Many people consider Ishmael the father of the Arab people and Isaac one of the forefathers of the Jews.

144

Drunk Lady in the Worship Center?

Distressed because she was unable to have children, Hannah poured out her heart to God at the Jewish worship center. The high priest, Eli, got the wrong idea. "Hannah prayed silently to the LORD for a long time. But her lips were moving, and Eli thought she was drunk" (1 Samuel 1:12 CEV).

"I'm not drunk," Hannah replied. "I've been praying all this time, telling the LORD about my problems" (verses 15-16 CEV).

Perhaps a bit embarrassed at his hasty judgment, Eli blessed Hannah. "May the God of Israel grant the request you have asked of him" (verse 17).

God did just that. Hannah gave birth to Samuel, who would grow up to become one of Israel's most revered prophets.

145

How to Shrink an Army

As far as God was concerned, Gideon's army of 32,000 was too big to attack a much larger invasion force. God wanted a strike force of just 300. "The LORD said to Gideon, 'I don't want the Israelites to brag that they saved themselves'" (Judges 7:2 NCV).

If a general is going to pick 300 men out of 32,000 to lead a covert military op against mega thousands of invaders, you'd think he'd pick the 300 best. Yet God gave Gideon some unique instructions for selecting his troops.

In Gideon's first pass at reducing the size of his army, he was to simply tell everyone who felt afraid to go home. Some 22,000 men with excellent survival instincts did just that—two-thirds of the army.

God used water to shrink the rest of Gideon's army to the point that they could fit in five tour buses. Gideon took them to a spring and asked them to drink. All but 300 of the men lay facedown and drank the water much like an animal would. The other 300 knelt and then scooped water with their hands.

Some scholars speculate that God directed Gideon to choose those men because that technique for drinking allowed them to keep an eye on their surroundings, which would suggest they were the more savvy warriors. That might be true, but it's just speculation.

146

How to Kill a King with a Wet Blanket

When a sick Syrian king asked Hazael, one of his officials, to go to a Jewish prophet and find out if he would get well, Hazael did as asked. But when he came back, he suffocated the king with a wet blanket.

The prophet Elijah had perhaps unwittingly provided the motive for the murder. "Hazael, the LORD has told me that you will be the next king of Syria" (2 Kings 8:13 CEV). Not taking any chances of missing his shot at wealth and power, Hazael made sure the prediction came true.

Ancient Assyrian records from what is now neighboring Iraq confirm that Hazael did not inherit his throne from King Benhadad, calling Hazael "the son of a nobody."

147

Heaven Can Wait

Even as late as Jesus's time, Jews still debated whether or not there was an afterlife.

The Old Testament often says that godly people simply went to the grave. "Heaven belongs to the LORD, but he gave the earth to people. Dead people do not praise the LORD; those in the grave are silent" (Psalm 115:16-17 NCV).

In Jesus's day, one group of Jews, the Pharisees, argued there was life after death. But another group, the Sadducees, said, "There is no resurrection or angels" (Acts 23:8).

The Jewish understanding of an afterlife seemed to evolve over the centuries.

Abraham and other folks in the earliest Bible times seemed to think that heaven was a blue dome above the earth, according to many Bible experts. It was blue because it contained water that fell when God opened heaven's windows.

By the time of Jesus, some Jews were writing about different levels of heaven. One Jewish writer in a book called 2 Enoch talked about the "seventh heaven." The apostle Paul referred to levels of heaven. "I was caught up to the third heaven fourteen years ago. Whether I was in my body or out of my body, I don't know" (2 Corinthians 12:2-4).

Whatever heaven is like, Jesus said it's not reserved for God alone. "I am going to prepare a place for you...Then you will also be where I am" (John 14:2-3 NIRV).

148

In Search of Purgatory

Most Protestants reject the Roman Catholic teaching about purgatory because it's not in the Protestant Bible.

The idea does appear in Bibles used by Catholic and Orthodox Christians. When a Jewish commander offered sacrifices for men killed in battle, "He made atonement for the dead, so that they might be delivered from their sin" (2 Maccabees 12:45).

Catholic and Orthodox Christians teach that purgatory—the word can mean "purge" or "cleanse"—is a place where Christians go after they die to purify themselves for heaven. One Bible writer named John, who said he had a vision of heaven, wrote, "Nothing unclean will enter it" (Revelation 21:27 NRSV).

As some Christians put it, believers who die with only minor unconfessed sins are relatively quickly ushered out of purgatory and sent on to heaven. Christians who committed more serious sins have to undergo more intense cleansing. The most serious unconfessed sins, such as rape and murder, lead to hell.

About 1000 years ago, many Catholic leaders used the belief in purgatory to raise money. They sold indulgences, which were a bit like fast-pass tickets out of purgatory. Fundraisers said if a person gave money to the church on behalf of a dead loved one, the loved one would go immediately to heaven. These donations funded some of the most beautiful buildings in Vatican City, including St. Peter's Basilica, where the pope addresses crowds.

Church reformers such as Martin Luther protested, saying the idea was exploitive nonsense. His protest jump-started the Protestant movement.

149

The First Martyred Disciple

Jewish King Herod Agrippa gave one of the apostles an unwanted claim to fame. "He had the apostle James (John's brother) killed with a sword," making him the first disciple to be martyred. Then, "when Herod saw how much this pleased the Jewish people, he also arrested Peter" (Acts 12:2-3).

Early church writers reported that almost every one of Jesus's original disciples died as martyrs. But the Bible reports only the death of James, the brother of John. James, John, and Peter seem to have been Jesus's three best friends.

After Peter's arrest and imprisonment, he escaped in the night with the help of an angel. "Suddenly, there was a bright light in the cell, and an angel of the Lord stood before Peter" (verse 7).

At daybreak there was a lot of commotion among the 16 soldiers assigned to guard him. "Herod interrogated the guards and sentenced them to death" (verse 19).

150

Death by Worms

Herod Agrippa I, appointed by Rome as king of the Jews a few years after Jesus's crucifixion, suffered a pretty terrible death.

He had just made a speech in Caesarea, on what is now Israel's Mediterranean coast. In Bible times, it was Rome's capital in this part of the Middle East. The crowd gave him quite a response. "They shouted, 'This is the voice of a god. It's not the voice of a man.' Right away an angel of the Lord struck Herod down. Herod had not given praise to God. So he was eaten by worms and died" (verses 21-23 NIRV).

What's odd about Herod's death is that it sounds very much like the way Roman history writers say his grandfather, Herod the Great, died. Jewish historian Josephus (about AD 37–100) said the symptoms of Herod the Great included "intense itching, painful intestinal problems, breathlessness, convulsions in every limb, and gangrene of the genitals," which attracted maggots.

Some physicians today speculate that Herod the Great's gangrene could have been caused by gonorrhea, persistent scratching, or an abdominal infection that spread to his groin.

151
Nightmare of Pilate's Wife

It may have been just a little after daybreak when Jesus found himself standing before Pilate, Roman governor of the region.

Jesus had just endured an all-night trial before the Jewish leaders. By around 5:30 a.m., the last of the high council showed up and concurred with the findings of the high priest. They agreed that Jesus had to die because he showed extreme disrespect for God by claiming to be God's Son. They led him to Pilate, the Roman governor, to be executed.

Pilate's wife must have awakened during her husband's trial of Jesus. "While court was still in session, Pilate's wife sent him a message: 'Don't get mixed up in judging this noble man. I've just been through a long and troubled night because of a dream about him'" (Matthew 27:19 MSG).

152
King of Jews: Not a Jew

By race, Herod the Great might better be described as an Arab.

He came from the non-Jewish nation of Idumea, known in the Old Testament as Edom—a nation in what is now Jordan. By New Testament times the Idumeans had migrated into what is now southern Israel.

Earlier, Jews had won a war of independence against Greek rulers who tried to impose their religion on them. The Jews quickly did the same for the people now under their control, forcing the Idumeans—including Herod's grandfather—to convert to the Jewish faith or die. So Herod, king of the Jews, was a Jew by conversion.

That was not Jewish enough to be king as far as many Jews of his day were concerned. At least that's the report we get from first-century historians, such as Josephus (about AD 37–100).

153
Secret Tunnel in Jerusalem

Jerusalem was built on the top of a ridge and surrounded by walls. There was no source of water for the people living inside those walls. They had to go outside the city to a spring on the slopes near the bottom of the ridge.

King Hezekiah was expecting an attack from Assyrians based in what is now Iraq. He knew that when they came to Jerusalem they would surround the city, cutting off the water supply. Not wanting his people to die of thirst, he arranged for miners to chisel a tunnel "that carried the water from Gihon Spring into the city of Jerusalem" (2 Chronicles 32:30 CEV).

Miners worked from both sides of the route, meeting somewhere in between. The tunnel stretches 582 yards (532 m). It was rediscovered in 1880, with the ancient stone plaque describing "the story of its cutting." Tourists today wade from one end of the tunnel to the other.

154

When God Changed His Mind

God told the prophet Isaiah to warn the ailing King Hezekiah he would soon die.

"Hezekiah turned toward the wall and prayed, 'Don't forget that I have been faithful to you, Lord. I have obeyed you with all my heart, and I do whatever you say is right.' After this, he cried hard" (2 Kings 20:2-3 CEV).

That's all it took. A few minutes later, God reversed himself, saying he'd give Hezekiah 15 more years.

What was it about Hezekiah's prayer that convinced God to reverse his decision? The Bible writer doesn't tell us. God simply says, "I heard you pray, and I saw you cry" (verse 5 CEV).

This story begs the question of why a God who is supposed to know everything would change his mind. It seems to suggest he doesn't know everything. Yet Bible writers say "he knows everything" (1 John 3:20).

Some theologians speculate that whatever happened during Hezekiah's prayer somehow changed Hezekiah—and that God changed his plans accordingly.

For whatever reason, and in that particular case, prayer made a difference of 15 years.

155

The Good King from Bad Stock

Hezekiah was lucky to have survived his father, Ahaz, who "sacrificed his son in the fire to another god" (2 Kings 16:3 NIRV).

In addition, Hezekiah was fortunate that he was Manasseh's father and not his son. "Manasseh also sacrificed his own son in the fire" (2 Kings 21:6).

Sandwiched between these two rotten-apple kings, Hezekiah not only manages to elude the stink, he comes out smelling sweet, earning the Bible's highest praise of any king: "Hezekiah trusted in the LORD, the God of Israel. There was no one like him among all the kings of Judah, either before or after his time. He remained faithful to the LORD in everything" (2 Kings 18:5-6).

156

When Jewish Worship Got Arab Help

The Arab and the Jew were business partners.

Hiram, king of Tyre (in modern-day Lebanon), provided King Solomon with top-grade lumber for the first Jewish temple—"as much cedar and cypress timber as Solomon desired" (1 Kings 5:10). "In return, Solomon sent him an annual payment of 100,000 bushels of wheat for his household and 110,000 gallons of pure olive oil" (verse 11). Hiram also sent builders to "prepare the timber and stone for the Temple" (verse 18).

Solomon later traded land for lumber to build his palace. He gave Hiram 20 cities in what is now northern Israel. But when Hiram went to visit the cities, he wasn't impressed. He named the land "Good for Nothing" (1 Kings 9:13 GWT).

157

Face-to-Face with God

God told Moses, "You may not look directly at my face, for no one may see me and live" (Exodus 33:20). But two folks seem to have come close.

One was Moses himself. God tells him, "I will hide you in the crevice of the rock and cover you with my hand until I have passed by. Then I will remove my hand and let you see me from behind" (verses 22-23). And in Moses's obituary, we read, "The LORD spoke face to face with him" (Deuteronomy 34:10 CEV).

The other was Jacob, who said, "I have seen God face to face, and I am still alive" (Genesis 32:30 CEV). He was talking about a mysterious man he wrestled all night. The Bible simply describes his opponent as a man. Yet this person admits that Jacob "fought with God" (verse 28)—if not in the overnight struggle, certainly in other ways.

Many Bible experts explain that this story and others that seem to portray God in the flesh talking with people are reporting manifestations of God, not God in all of his glory.

158

God's Spirit on the Job

In Old Testament times, the Holy Spirit seemed to function as a spiritual Special Forces operative.

He could be called into action to help one person for a lifetime, as he did with King David. "The Spirit of the LORD came powerfully upon David from that day on" (1 Samuel 16:13). The Spirit could also be withdrawn from the person, which is what happened with King Saul. "The Spirit of the LORD had left Saul" (verse 14).

The prophet Joel proclaimed that one day, God would give

his Spirit to everyone: "I will pour out my Spirit upon all people" (Joel 2:28). In New Testament times, Christians taught that Joel's prophecy was fulfilled on the Day of Pentecost, when the Spirit's arrival fired up the disciples, who started telling others about Jesus in Jerusalem, the very city where Jewish leaders had arranged for the execution of Jesus just a few weeks earlier.

As Peter explained, "What you see was predicted long ago by the prophet Joel...Each of you must repent of your sins and turn to God...Then you will receive the gift of the Holy Spirit" (Acts 2:16,38).

159
Wild and Crazy Driver

Jehu apparently had a reputation as a reckless driver. A lookout on the walls of Jezreel, a ridgetop city in what is now northern Israel, easily identified him from long distance. "It must be Jehu... for he's driving like a madman" (2 Kings 9:20).

Jehu commanded a chariot corps along Israel's northeastern border. When the prophet Elisha anointed him as Israel's future king, Jehu mobilized his troops and led them on a charge about 40 miles (64 km) west to Jezreel. That's where Israel's King Joram was recovering from wounds suffered in a battle.

The city watchman spotted Jehu in a cloud of dust, and alerted the king—who apparently thought Jehu was coming to report an invasion. Instead, Jehu assassinated him on the spot. "Jehu drew his bow and shot Joram between the shoulders. The arrow pierced his heart" (2 Kings 9:24).

Jehu also killed the queen mother, Jezebel. After that, he assassinated all the potential heirs to the throne. Then he declared himself the God-appointed, prophet-anointed king of Israel.

160

Wanted: Wife for a Momma's Boy

With his mom three years dead, 40-year-old Isaac apparently remained inconsolable. Father Abraham decided to treat Isaac's symptoms with a wife.

Abraham did not want a local Canaanite daughter-in-law. He wanted a relative.

He sent his most trusted servant north to Haran, in what is now Turkey. That's where some of Abraham's relatives lived and where Abraham once lived. The servant came back with Rebekah, granddaughter of Abraham's brother.

As the Bible tells it, she was just what the doctor ordered. "Isaac brought Rebekah into the tent…She became his wife, and he loved her. So Isaac was comforted after his mother died" (Genesis 24:67 NIRV).

161

Calling in the Baby-Making B Team

Sarah was in her mid-seventies (about ten years younger than Abraham) when she resigned herself to the fact that she would never have a baby. "Sarai said to Abram, 'The LORD has prevented me from having children. Go and sleep with my servant'…This happened ten years after Abram had settled in the land of Canaan" (Genesis 16:2-3).

The plan worked. "Abram was eighty-six years old when Ishmael was born" (verse 16).But to Sarah's happy surprise, she gave birth to Isaac roughly 14 years later, when she was 90 years old and Abraham was getting started on his second century.

162

A Name Tough to Spell in Kindergarten

Isaiah gave his son the longest name in the Bible.

"The LORD said, 'Call him Maher-shalal-hash-baz. For before this child is old enough to say "Papa" or "Mama," the king of Assyria will carry away both the abundance of Damascus and the riches of Samaria'" (Isaiah 8:3-4).

We can only hope they gave him a nickname. Swifty would have worked. That's pretty close to the meaning of the first part of his Hebrew name: Maher. His name is a Hebrew phrase that means "swift to plunder and quick to spoil."

Isaiah, like the prophet Hosea, used his children's names to make prophetic points. He wanted King Ahaz of Judah, the southern Jewish nation, to know that Judah did not need Assyria's help to fight off coalition forces of Syria and the northern Jewish nation of Israel. Those two enemies of Judah, Isaiah predicted, would be conquered and looted of their war spoils before Swifty was old enough to talk.

The king ignored Isaiah's advice and recruited Assyria anyhow. Assyria crushed Judah's enemies but at great cost to Judah. The Assyrians took Judah's sacred temple treasures as payment.

163

Three Years Naked

The prophet Isaiah spent three years naked on the streets of Jerusalem.

He was warning the Jews not to depend on Egyptian allies to help them. "This is a sign—a symbol of the terrible troubles I will bring upon Egypt and Ethiopia. For the king of Assyria will take away the Egyptians and Ethiopians as prisoners. He will make them walk naked and barefoot, both young and old, their buttocks bared, to the shame of Egypt" (Isaiah 20:3-4).

Some other prophets, such as Ezekiel, also sometimes acted out their prophecies. This proved to be a great way to help the Jews remember what they had said. That's likely one reason the stories ended up in the Bible.

Walking naked—perhaps in a loincloth, perhaps not—Isaiah was trying to convince King Hezekiah not to sign an alliance with Egypt. Many rulers in this part of the Middle East were worried about the encroaching Assyrian Empire, based in what is now Iraq. These small kingdoms were forging alliances to protect themselves.

Isaiah convinced Hezekiah to trust God instead of the Egyptian army.

Wise advice.

When Assyrians invaded in 701 BC, they surrounded Jerusalem. Egyptians rushed north to fight off the Assyrians before they reached the Egyptian homeland. The Assyrians crushed the Egyptian army.

Yet the Assyrians were unable to defeat Jerusalem. They abruptly gave up the siege and left for home. "The angel of the LORD went out to the Assyrian camp and killed 185,000 Assyrian soldiers" (Isaiah 37:36). Greek historian Herodotus said mice carried some kind of plague that made the soldiers sick on their way to Egypt. Some scholars say that sounds like bubonic plague.

164

When Israel Was a Man

Before Israel was a nation, Israel was a man.

Actually, that was his second name. God had renamed him: "Your name will no longer be Jacob...From now on you will be called Israel, because you have fought with God and with men and have won" (Genesis 32:28).

Jacob was on his way back home to what is now Israel for an unnerving reunion with Esau, the twin brother he had exploited and robbed 20 years earlier. Just before crossing the border marked by the Jordan River, Jacob managed to get himself into an all-night wrestling match with a mysterious man that many Bible scholars say was either an angel or a manifestation of God himself.

At daybreak, the mystery man broke free, and Jacob was renamed Israel.

Bible experts can't agree on exactly what the name means except to say that it has something to do with fighting. Some scholars say it means "God fights," perhaps implying that God will fight on behalf of his people. Or it might mean "someone who fights with God," a prediction of how God's people would resist him for many centuries.

165

Jews Worship Gold Calves, Part 2

That brief moment during the Exodus, when Moses was up on Mount Sinai, wasn't the only time Jews worshipped a gold calf.

Centuries later, when Israel split into two countries, King Jeroboam set up a gold calf in Samaria, capital of the northern kingdom. He told his people, "You won't have to go to Jerusalem [in the southern kingdom] to worship anymore. Here are your gods who rescued you from Egypt" (1 Kings 12:28 CEV).

Bible experts speculate that King Jeroboam wasn't especially concerned about making worship more convenient for his people. Instead, they say, he was more likely concerned about staying alive.

If his northern Jews continued their regular pilgrimages south to Jerusalem, they might one day long for a reunification of the nation. If that happened, Jeroboam would be out of a job. Kings in the southern nation were considered legit only if they descended from David. He didn't.

166
Rachel's Request: Aphrodisiac

Mandrakes were roots that sometimes looked a bit like a human torso with arms and legs. Maybe that's why some people in ancient times considered the root a baby maker.

One of the times it shows up in the Bible, it actually works—though not quite as expected.

Unable to have children, Rachel made a swap with her very fertile sister, Leah. One of Leah's sons had found some mandrake roots, so Rachel made a trade: "I will let Jacob sleep with you tonight if you give me some of the mandrakes" (Genesis 30:15). She got the roots, and Leah got an extra night to sleep with Jacob.

Leah also got pregnant.

Rachel didn't.

Mandrake, zero. Sperm, one.

167

Wrestling God

It's one of the most puzzling stories in the Bible. As Jacob and his family approached what is now Israel—for a tense reunion with his twin brother Esau, whom he had exploited and robbed 20 years earlier—Jacob sent his family across the Jordan River. But he stayed behind.

"This left Jacob all alone in the camp, and a man came and wrestled with him until the dawn began to break" (Genesis 32:24).

There's no indication who the man he wrestled was or why the man and Jacob got into a fight. As the story unfolds, however, it seems clear that Jacob comes to believe the man is a celestial being, perhaps God. That would explain why Jacob…

- Insists, "I will not let you go unless you bless me" (verse 26).

- "Named the place Peniel (which means 'face of God')" (verse 30).

- Declares, "I have seen God face to face, yet my life has been spared" (verse 30).

168

Favorite Son

Parents throughout the ancient Middle East, by custom, treated their firstborn son like the king of the kids—even if the father had a second (and better loved) wife. "When the man divides his inheritance, he may not give the larger inheritance to his younger son… He must recognize the rights of his oldest son, the son of the wife he does not love, by giving him a double portion" (Deuteronomy 21:16-17).

In Jewish tradition, the oldest son got twice as much of the family estate as any other brother. When Esau traded his birthright for a bowl of soup, this seems to have been what he was giving to his younger brother Jacob—perhaps in addition to the right of the oldest son to lead the extended family after their father died.

169

Blessings and Curses: Words You Can't Take Back

Jacob's father Isaac—more than 100 years old and blind—mistakenly thought he was dying. So he told his oldest and favorite son, Esau (Jacob's twin) to hunt some fresh meat and fix him a meal. Isaac promised to give Esau the customary deathbed blessing after his meal.

This blessing was more than a prayer. Many of God's people saw it as a way to invoke God's power, releasing the energy to make things happen—for better or worse, depending on whether the words were a blessing or a curse. Once spoken, the words were alive; there was no way to kill them.

Rebekah, Jacob and Esau's mother, convinced Jacob to cheat his big brother out of their father's deathbed blessing. "My son, listen carefully to what I want you to do" (Genesis 27:8 CEV). Why? Perhaps because "Isaac loved Esau...but Rebekah loved Jacob" (Genesis 25:28).

Or maybe Rebekah was just trying to help along a prediction God had made when she was carrying the twins. "The sons in your womb will become two nations. From the very beginning, the two nations will be rivals. One nation will be stronger than the other; and your older son will serve your younger son" (Genesis 25:23).

Isaac's blessing for Jacob—which he had intended for Esau—included that very promise: "May you be the master over your brothers" (Genesis 27:29).

170

The Man Who Kissed the Woman

Lovers in the Song of Songs talk a good kiss, but in the entire Bible there's only one story of a man actually kissing the woman he will marry. "Jacob kissed Rachel, and he wept aloud" (Genesis 29:11).

There may have been more relief than romance in Jacob's first kiss of Rachel.

Jacob had been running for his life for about 500 miles (800 km). After Jacob cheated his twin brother, Esau, out of their father's deathbed blessing, Esau vowed to kill Jacob. So Jacob hightailed it to what is now the southern border of Turkey. His mother, Rebekah, sent him there to live with relatives. Rebekah's brother, Laban, lived there near the village of Haran.

After traveling for what must have been the better part of a month, and realizing he had finally and safely reached his extended family, he was overjoyed. So he kissed his cousin when he met her out in the field watering her father's flock. It probably didn't hurt that she was a looker with "a beautiful figure and a lovely face" (Genesis 29:17).

Jacob later married Rachel.

171

God's Odd Choice of a Leader

On the run from his twin brother, who had vowed to kill him, Jacob had a dream. He saw God at the top of a stairway leading to heaven. In that dream, God promised to bless him and make his descendants a blessing to all nations.

Jacob was an odd choice for a blessing like that. At this point in the story, he was a jerk, with no redemptive qualities to his character except that he was a good cook. "Esau hated his brother Jacob because he had stolen the blessing that was supposed to be his" (Genesis 27:41 CEV).

In other words, God rewards the bad guy in the story. That's what it sounds like. Jacob gets God's gracious blessing after…

- Exploiting the hunger of his older twin brother, Esau, giving him a bowl of stew for an ungodly price—Esau's birthright as the oldest son (a double share of their father's estate).

- Stealing his father's deathbed blessing, which was intended for the oldest son, by pretending to be Esau.

Readers are left to draw the conclusion that God must have seen something in Jacob that no one else could have imagined.

Twenty years later, Jacob finally returned home and reconciled with his brother.

172
How to Raise Spotted Sheep

Jacob used the science of what sounds like an old wives' tale to grow his herds. His father-in-law paid him to tend his flocks by letting him keep all the speckled or black sheep and goats. So he wanted lots of those critters, and he wanted to breed them strong.

He paired the strongest animals when it came time for them to mate—the science of selective breeding.

But then, "Jacob took branches...He made white stripes on them by peeling off the bark...He placed them so they would be right in front of the flocks when they came to drink. The flocks... mated in front of the branches" (Genesis 30:37-39 NIRV). The science of an old wives' tale. Or so it would seem.

There's plenty of evidence to support the idea that strong sheep and goats are more likely to produce strong lambs and kids. But there doesn't seem to be anything to support the idea that if they mate while looking at striped colors, they'll produce spotted or streaked lambs and kids.

But as the Genesis writer tells it, the science of the old wives tale worked. "Jacob became very wealthy, with large flocks of sheep and goats" (verse 43).

Most Bible scholars attribute Jacob's success to God and not to his use of questionable science.

173
Wives for Sale

Men in Bible times didn't actually buy their wives—at least in most cases. But it was customary for them to give a gift to the bride's father. Women were considered property, so the father needed to be compensated for the loss of a household worker.

Jacob didn't have anything to offer Rachel's father, Laban. So they struck a deal—Jacob would work for Laban for seven years.

On the wedding night, Laban pulled a switcheroo. Jacob woke up the next morning with the wrong wife—Rachel's older and apparently homely sister, Leah. Laban explained that it was customary for his people to marry off the oldest daughter first. But apparently it wasn't customary to mention the custom ahead of time. Laban made Jacob a deal. "I will give you Rachel to marry also. But you must serve me another seven years" (Genesis 29:27 NCV).

Jacob agreed, as long as he could go ahead and marry Rachel after the traditional week of celebrating his marriage to Leah. So within the span of a week, Jacob got married twice.

174
Surrogate Moms Build Israel's 12 Tribes

As the Bible tells it, Jacob's home life seemed like a perpetual baby-making competition between his two sister-wives, Leah and Rachel.

"When the LORD saw that Jacob loved Rachel more than Leah, he made it possible for Leah to have children, but not Rachel" (Genesis 29:31 NCV).

Leah had four sons, one after the other: Reuben, Simeon, Levi, and Judah.

When Rachel realized she couldn't have kids, she asked her slave girl to provide Jacob with children on her behalf. Middle Eastern custom allowed this. (It was a man's world.) Not to be outdone, Leah did the same. So four of Israel's 12 tribes were founded by men born to surrogate mothers. "Jacob had...two sons by Rachel's slave girl Bilhah...two sons by Leah's slave girl Zilpah" (Genesis 35:22, 25-26 NCV).

Leah had two more sons, and finally, Rachel gave birth to Joseph and Benjamin—dying as she gave birth to Benjamin.

175
Father of the Jews: Stuffed

Jacob, one of Israel's founding fathers, was embalmed instead of buried.

He died in Egypt, about 200 miles (320 km) from his home in what is now Israel. But his last wish was, "Bury me with my father and grandfather...in Canaan" (Genesis 49:29-30). Embalming made it easier to transport the body.

Joseph honored his father's wish. He had the Egyptians embalm him. They removed his internal organs and dried the corpse by covering it with salt for 40 days. The Egyptians mourned Jacob for 70 days, and then Joseph took his father home for burial, accompanied by an entourage of Egyptian officials and Jacob's entire extended family. The journey to what is now Israel may have taken two or three weeks.

Joseph followed in his father's steps. "Joseph made the sons of Israel swear an oath...'Take my bones with you.' So Joseph died at the age of 110. The Egyptians embalmed him" (Genesis 50:25-26). Jacob and Joseph are the only two Jews identified in the Bible as getting embalmed.

Joseph's mummy remained in Egypt until Moses led the Jewish people home about 400 years later. "The people of Israel lived in Egypt for 430 years" (Exodus 12:40).

176

Jesus Called Them "Sons of Thunder"

Jesus nicknamed two of his disciples, brothers James and John, the Sons of Thunder (Mark 3:17). Was it because of their chutzpah?

It's just a guess, but many scholars suggest that Jesus nicknamed James and John Sons of Thunder because God gave them an extra helping of boldness. Here are three examples.

- *Fireball.* "A Samaritan village…did not welcome Jesus. That was because he was heading for Jerusalem. The disciples James and John saw this. They asked, 'Lord, do you want us to call down fire from heaven to destroy them?'" (Luke 9:52-54 NIRV).

- *Chutzpah.* "James and John came to Jesus…'Teacher,' they said, 'we would like to ask a favor of you…Let one of us sit at your right hand in your glorious kingdom. Let the other one sit at your left hand'" (Mark 10:35,37 NIRV).

- *First to die.* "King Herod got it into his head to go after some of the church members. He murdered James, John's brother" (Acts 12:1-2 MSG). James is Jesus's only disciple whose death is reported in the Bible.

177

Family Intervention for Crazy Jesus

Jesus healed people. That was the main attraction for crowds, at least initially. He also exorcised people of demons.

It might be a fair guess that this is what pulled the trigger on his family's attempted intervention. Immediately after Mark reported Jesus sending out his apostles to preach and to exorcise demons, he added, "Jesus went back home...When Jesus's family heard what he was doing, they thought he was crazy and went to get him under control" (Mark 3:20-21 CEV).

John, another Gospel writer, dittoed the idea that Jesus's family had not yet gotten on board with his ministry. "Even Jesus' own brothers had not yet become his followers" (John 7:5 CEV).

178

The Jesus Dynasty

In a day when kings ruled along family lines, it should probably come as no surprise that when the King of kings left the planet, people chose his closest relative to replace him as leader of the Christian movement—James, probably Jesus's oldest brother (Galatians 1:19).

Jesus had four brothers: "James, Joseph, Simon, and Judas" (Matthew 13:55). James is listed first, as though he's the oldest of the four.

When the first generation of Christians couldn't decide whether non-Jewish followers of Jesus needed to follow the Jewish laws, James convened a meeting of leaders in Jerusalem. After hearing the testimony of other leaders, including Peter and Paul, James made the judgment call that non-Jews did not have to follow Jewish laws (Acts 15:19-21).

Jesus's dynasty, if we could call it that, seemed to end with James. First-century Jewish historian Josephus said Jewish leaders condemned James for breaking their law. They pushed him from a high spot in the temple and finished him off with stones and clubs.

179
Who Stole the Trinity?

Here's how the New King James Version refers to the Trinity, in a way much like its older cousin, the King James Version. All other Bibles drop the italicized part.

"For there are three that bear witness *in heaven: the Father, the Word, and the Holy Spirit; and these three are one. And there are three that bear witness on earth*: the Spirit, the water, and the blood; and these three agree as one" (1 John 5:7 NKJV). *Word* is a nickname John often applied to Jesus because in Greek, the original language of the New Testament, it refers to the source of all life.

Here's how the Bible verse reads in another translation. "There are three that give witness about Jesus. They are the Holy Spirit, the baptism of Jesus and his death. And the three of them agree" (NIRV).

Newer Bible translations drop the phrase about the Trinity because it doesn't show up in the oldest and most reliable copies of the New Testament—copies many centuries older than the ones scholars used to translate the 1611 King James Version. (For more background, see number 65, "Who Stole John 5:4?")

Scholars have many theories about how the mysterious phrase popped up in more recent Latin and Greek copies of the New Testament. One is that an editor added it to help explain this confusing verse—perhaps as a note in the margin that eventually worked its way into the verse.

Most scholars agree that the extra words don't seem to belong in this verse. But most do agree that the idea of a Trinity comes from Jesus himself in the marching orders he gives his followers: "Make disciples of all nations. Baptize them in the name of the Father and of the Son and of the Holy Spirit" (Matthew 28:19 NIRV).

180

Teenage King's Only Legacy: Surrender

Jehoiachin found himself in the wrong place at the wrong time. He was just 18 years old when he inherited his father's throne in Jerusalem. The bad news: Babylonian King Nebuchadnezzar was already on his way to lay siege to the city.

In what amounted to an act of war, Jehoiachin's father had refused to pay taxes to the Babylonian Empire. Then he died and left his son to face the consequences. Three months later, "King Jehoiachin...surrendered to the Babylonians" (2 Kings 24:12). King Nebuchadnezzar pillaged the city, palace, and temple. That may have been when the Jews forever lost their most sacred relic—the Ark of the Covenant, a gold-plated chest containing the original Ten Commandments.

Nebuchadnezzar installed a new king and took Jehoiachin captive to Babylon.

181

Lucky Shot

Ahab, king of the northern Jewish nation of Israel, is best known today as husband of infamous Queen Jezebel, who tried to wipe out the Jewish religion by killing all the prophets.

But in his own time, he was respected as a skilled military leader. Twice he defeated Syrian invaders. And once he fought in a coalition that stopped the Iraq-based Assyrian Empire in their push toward Israel.

He died in a freak accident during a battle while trying to recapture Jewish land east of the Jordan River in what is now the Arab country of Jordan. "During the fighting a soldier shot an arrow without even aiming, and it hit Ahab where two pieces of his armor joined. He shouted to his chariot driver, 'I've been hit! Get me out of here!'" (1 Kings 22:34 CEV).

He managed to remain propped up in his chariot all day, watching the battle. But "he bled so much that the bottom of the chariot was covered with blood, and by evening he was dead" (verse 35 CEV).

182

The King Wore a Bull's-Eye

Ahab, king of the northern Jewish nation of Israel, figured out a creative way to keep himself alive in an upcoming battle—pin a bull's-eye on someone else.

Ahab had joined forces with Jehoshaphat, king of the southern Jewish nation of Judah. They were prepping to cross the Jordan River and reclaim Jewish land in what is now the Arab country of Jordan.

Ahab asked his prophets if the gods promised him victory. The Lord's prophet Micaiah predicted not only that they would lose the battle but that Ahab would lose his life.

Ahab worked up a plan to protect himself. He told King Jehoshaphat, "As we go into battle, I will disguise myself so no one will recognize me, but you wear your royal robes" (1 Kings 22:30). Bull's-eye.

Jehoshaphat probably would not have agreed to that had he known the standing orders for the enemy soldiers: "Attack only the king of Israel. Don't bother with anyone else!" (verse 31).

Ahab's plan appeared to work. "When the…chariot commanders saw Jehoshaphat in his royal robes, they went after him" (verse 32). But when Jehoshaphat saw the entire enemy army charging toward him, he screamed. The Bible doesn't say what, but whatever it was, the enemies stopped chasing him when they realized they had the wrong guy, who, given the situation, may have hit high C.

Ahab died in that battle, killed by a stray arrow that penetrated the seam of his armor.

183

Seventy Heads in a Pile

A chariot commander named Jehu ordered 70 human heads in baskets, to go.

Kings who fought their way to the throne by leading a coup and assassinating the previous king, as Jehu did, generally wanted to make sure that none of the dead king's relatives survived to later challenge his right to rule. Ahab's family dynasty—which had started with his father, Omri—was on its third generation. Ahab's son Joram ruled the northern Jewish nation of Israel.

Jehu killed Joram and the queen mother, Jezebel, while they

were relaxing at their summer palace in Jezreel. Then he sent orders to leaders in the capital city of Samaria. "Bring me the heads of the descendants of Ahab" (2 Kings 10:6 CEV)—or prepare for battle.

The leaders chose option one. Jehu piled the 70 heads beside the city gate in Jezreel.

184

The Hero Who Sacrificed His Daughter

Jephthah, a Jewish hero from the time of Samson and Gideon, sacrificed his daughter—his only child. A God thing, he thought.

"Jephthah made a vow to the LORD. He said, 'If you give me victory over the Ammonites, I will give to the LORD whatever comes out of my house to meet me when I return in triumph. I will sacrifice it as a burnt offering'" (Judges 11:30-31).

It was a stupid vow to begin with. For two reasons.

First, what did he expect would come out of his house to greet him when he returned from war? The family goat?

Second, it was illegal. Jewish law stipulated, "Never sacrifice your son or daughter as a burnt offering" (Deuteronomy 18:10).

185

I Don't Wanna Be a Prophet

Jeremiah may have been barely a teenager when God called him to become a prophet. He tried to talk God out of it. "I can't speak for you! I'm too young!" (Jeremiah 1:6).

Bible experts say the Hebrew word describing him is probably best translated as "boy." Given the context of the story, he might have been about 12 or 13—not yet considered a Jewish adult.

Jeremiah was just one of several prophets who did not want to become a prophet. Prophecy wasn't what you would call a fun job. People had a hard time warming up to prophets who delivered bad news, which is what most prophets in Bible times did.

Other prophets who didn't want to be prophets include…

- *Moses.* When God told Moses to confront Pharaoh, Moses replied, "O LORD, I'm not very good with words…I get tongue-tied, and my words get tangled…LORD, please! Send anyone else" (Exodus 4:10,13).

- *Jonah.* When God told Jonah to go to Nineveh, capital of the Assyrian Empire, "Jonah got up and went in the opposite direction" (Jonah 1:3).

186
The Rewritten Book of the Bible

The first draft of the book of Jeremiah got shredded and burned by the king.

Jeremiah had dictated his prophecy to a scribe named Baruch and ordered him to read it to worshippers at the temple. In the scroll, Jeremiah predicted the fall of the Jewish nation.

Palace officials took the scroll and read it to the king, who was warming himself beside a fire. He didn't like what he heard.

"Each time Jehudi a palace official finished reading three or four columns, the king took a knife and cut off that section of the scroll. He then threw it into the fire, section by section, until the whole scroll was burned up" (Jeremiah 36:23).

When Jeremiah heard what the king did, he hired Baruch to

help him produce a new and improved prophecy—adding an in-your-face warning for the king: "None of your descendants will ever be king of Judah" (verse 30 CEV).

After the king died, Babylonian invaders from what is now Iraq dethroned his son and appointed a Jewish king they thought would be more loyal to them.

The Bible book of Jeremiah comes from the second draft that the prophet dictated.

187

David's Great-Great-Grandma, the Hooker

King David's great-great-grandmother was perhaps the most famous hooker in the Bible.

Matthew doesn't come right out and say that Boaz's mother was Rahab the prostitute of Jericho, but many Bible experts say it's a fair guess. Otherwise, they say, Matthew would not have mentioned her in his Gospel. But he does: "Rahab was Boaz's mother. Boaz was the father of Obed…Obed was the father of Jesse. And Jesse was the father of King David" (Matthew 1:5-6 NIRV).

Speculation is that Matthew included her name in the genealogy of Jesus because he figured his readers would know which Rahab he was talking about. She was the Jericho local who turned on her own people by orchestrating the escape of two Jewish spies Joshua sent into the town. "Joshua spared Rahab the prostitute and her relatives…And she lives among the Israelites to this day" (Joshua 6:25).

188

The Bible's Most Remarkable Prediction About Jesus

Isaiah 53 is known as the Suffering Servant passage for good reason. It talks about a mysterious servant who suffers because of what others have done wrong. Sounds like Jesus, many scholars say.

Much of this short chapter reads like a remarkable prediction about Jesus—accurate enough that some have wondered if it was written after the time of Jesus—as history passed off as prophecy. "The servant was pierced because we had sinned…His wounds have healed us…His body was buried in the tomb of rich man" (Isaiah 53:5,9 NIRV).

It's not history. It was written before Jesus. The passage is in an ancient copy of Isaiah found in the famous Dead Sea Scrolls. It dates to about 125 BC.

Christians say they see Jesus in the chapter, but Jews say they see a description of the suffering that Jewish people have endured.

Here are a few other excerpts that many say seem to point to Jesus (all from the NIRV):

- "Men looked down on him. They didn't accept him. He knew all about sorrow and suffering" (verse 3).
- "He suffered the things we should have suffered. He took on himself the pain that should have been ours" (verse 4).
- "He was beaten down and made to suffer…He was led away like a sheep to be killed" (verse 7).
- "He was punished for the sins of my people" (verse 8).
- "He was killed even though he hadn't harmed anyone" (verse 9).
- "The LORD says, 'It was my plan to crush him and cause him to suffer. I made his life a guilt offering to pay for sin'" (verse 10).

189

How to Scare a Roman Soldier

As Matthew tells the story of Jesus's resurrection, it's not clear if the Roman soldiers guarding the tomb actually saw him walk out. It sounds like they fainted before that, when a glowing angel showed up.

> After the Sabbath, at dawn on the first day of the week…There was a violent earthquake, for an angel of the Lord came down from heaven and, going to the tomb, rolled back the stone and sat on it. His appearance was like lightning, and his clothes were white as snow. The guards were so afraid of him that they shook and became like dead men (Matthew 28:1-4 TNIV).

Soldiers stood on guard because Jesus had predicted he would rise from the dead on the third day. Jewish leaders who had orchestrated his execution feared that his disciples might steal the body and claim he did what he said he would do.

In fact, that's the story Jewish leaders bribed the soldiers to tell. "You are to say, 'His disciples came during the night and stole him away while we were asleep'" (Matthew 28:13 TNIV).

190

Pretty Dead

When Queen Mother Jezebel heard she was about to get assassinated, she reached for her makeup.

Jezebel and her son, King Joram, were at their summer palace in the northern Israel city of Jezreel when a chariot corps commander named Jehu led his men on a charge to the city.

King Joram rode out to meet him, fearing Jehu and his men had come to warn of an invasion.

Nope. Jehu shot the king dead with an arrow to the heart.

The queen mother must have gotten the word right away. "When Jezebel heard that Jehu had arrived in Jezreel, she made herself up—put on eyeshadow and arranged her hair—and posed seductively at the window" (2 Kings 9:30 MSG). When Jehu arrived, this former queen of mean remained true to her style. She yelled down at him, "Have you come in peace, you murderer?" (verse 31).

Jehu yelled to her servants an order they seemed all too eager to obey: "Throw her down!" (verse 33).

Her blood splattered against the palace wall. Like the captain of crunch, Jehu drove over her with his chariot. Then he went in the palace to get a bite to eat. When he came back outside, he discovered the dogs had been getting a bite to eat as well.

"When they went out to bury her, they found only her skull, her feet, and her hands" (verse 35). Apparently, she wasn't finger-lickin' good.

191

King David Wasn't a Kind Uncle

In a dying wish, King David asked his son Solomon to please kill David's nephew. David had his reasons.

After King Saul died, Saul's general, Abner, worked out an agreement with David. They would unite their two armies under the leadership of David. Abner never got the chance.

Joab was David's nephew and general. When Abner was on his way back to his army, "Joab and his brother Abishai killed Abner" (2 Samuel 3:30). It was a revenge killing. Abner had killed one of Joab's other brothers in battle.

Years later, Joab also assassinated David's oldest son, Absalom. In fairness to Joab, Absalom had launched a coup against his own father. Fleeing the lost battle, Absalom managed to get his long hair caught in the branch of an oak tree. The branch yanked him off his mule and left him hanging there like a nut.

David had given orders not to kill Absalom. Joab couldn't resist. "Joab...took three daggers and plunged them into Absalom's heart" (2 Samuel 18:14).

At the end of David's life, he made this last request of his son concerning Joab: "Don't let him live to become an old man. Don't let him die peacefully" (1 Kings 2:6 NIRV).

Solomon's men executed Joab as he frantically clutched the altar at Jerusalem's worship center, perhaps hoping he would get something he never seemed to give—mercy.

192

Slave Lady Who Outsmarted Her King

Jochebed, the mother of Moses, outsmarted the king of Egypt when he ordered that all newborn Jewish boys be thrown into the Nile River. "She got a basket that was made out of the stems of tall grass. She coated it with tar. Then she placed the child in it. She put the basket in the tall grass that grew along the bank of the Nile River" (Exodus 2:3 NIRV).

Jochebed put her boy in the river, like the king ordered. But she made sure her boy floated. Even better, she arranged for him to drop anchor at the very spot where the princess bathed. What princess could resist a newborn baby?

Jochebed had also arranged for her daughter, Miriam, to be nearby—close enough to make a suggestion to the princess. "Do you want me to go and get one of the Hebrew women? She could nurse the baby for you" (verse 7 NIRV).

Jochebed got the job—with a bonus. As the princess put it, "Take this baby. Nurse him for me. I'll pay you" (verse 9 NIRV).

Jochebed got paid to be Moses's mother.

193

Baal: Gone to the Potty

Elijah had challenged all 850 false prophets in the northern Jewish nation of Israel to a "pray off." Winner take all. The God who could send down fire from the sky to burn up the sacrificed animal would be the God of Israel.

Baal's prophets prayed all morning. No luck.

> They prayed to Baal from morning until noon…But there wasn't any reply…
>
> At noon Elijah began to tease them. "Shout louder!" he said. "I'm sure Baal is a god! Perhaps he has too much to think about. Or maybe he has gone to the toilet. Or perhaps he's away on a trip. Maybe he's sleeping. You might have to wake him up" (1 Kings 18:26-27 NIRV).

(For the rest of the story, see number 67, "Battle of the Gods on Mount Carmel." Spoiler alert: God won.)

194

Jonah, the Unhappy Savior

Jonah is one of the few prophets in the Bible who actually got the job done. He delivered God's message to the Assyrian city of Nineveh in what is now northern Iraq. "Forty days from now Nineveh will be destroyed!" (Jonah 3:4). The people believed what he said and repented of their sins.

Because of that, God changed his plans for the city. Jonah's message saved "more than 120,000 people" (Jonah 4:11).

But rather than being happy about the turn of events, Jonah felt as if God's mercy made him look like a liar. "This change of plans greatly upset Jonah, and he became very angry. So he complained to the LORD about it…'Just kill me now, LORD! I'd rather be dead than alive if what I predicted will not happen'" (verses 1-3).

Oddly enough, the story ends with Jonah pouting like a spoiled little brat and God asking, Why can't I show mercy to this important city?

This startling conclusion to the book—along with other features in the writing, such as the fact that there's only one prophecy, and it doesn't come true—leads some scholars to speculate that the story of Jonah is a parable. Most Christians, however, say they read the story as an event from history.

195
Jonah, 40 Leagues Under the Sea

Forget the urban legend of a man on a whaling ship getting swallowed by a whale and later being cut free by his crew. That story showed up on April 12, 1896, in the *New York World*, a newspaper published by Joseph Pulitzer of journalism's Pulitzer Prize fame. But the story was a hoax.

The name of the whaler, James Bartley, did not show up on the list of crewmen sailing on the ship, *Star of the East*. And the captain's wife confirmed that one Mr. Bartley never sailed with her husband. (The captain had died by the time reporters got around to checking their facts.)

Many Bible experts say Jonah's story might be a parable, partly because of the writing style and the story's abrupt, surprise ending—a feature of Jesus's parables. But also because of this fish story. "The LORD had arranged for a great fish to swallow Jonah. And Jonah was inside the fish for three days and three nights" (Jonah 1:17).

Ocean critter experts say the only swimmer large enough to swallow man is a great white shark. Even the largest known whale—the blue whale, which doesn't usually swim in the Mediterranean Sea—can swallow an object only about the diameter of a dinner plate.

Still, most Christians read the story as a matter of fact. Many argue that if a fish didn't exist that could swallow a man and hold him for three days, the God of creation could have made one.

196
Two for the Promised Land

Of all the adults Moses led out of Egypt for the Promised Land, only two lived long enough to make it their home. "The LORD had told the Israelites they would all die in the desert, and the only two left were Caleb…and Joshua" (Numbers 26:65 NCV).

The question is, why?

The answer is in the report they brought back after scouting out the Promised Land. Moses sent out 12 scouts, one from each of Israel's 12 tribes, to explore what is now Israel. Moses wanted intel on the people and the fortifications the Jews would have to overcome. Joshua and Caleb were the only two scouts who urged the Jews to press on with their invasion.

Speaking for both of them, Caleb said, "Let's go at once to take the land…We can certainly conquer it!" (Numbers 13:30).

The remaining 10 scouts disagreed. "The people who live there are fierce, their cities are huge and well fortified…We even saw the Nephilim giants…Alongside them we felt like grasshoppers" (verses 28,33 MSG).

Terrified by this report, the Jews refused to go any further. God sentenced them to 40 years in the badlands. "You have insulted me, and none of you men who are over twenty years old will enter the land that I solemnly promised to give you as your own—only Caleb and Joshua will go in" (Numbers 14:29-30 CEV).

197

Shocking Discovery in the Jewish Temple

While renovating the Jerusalem temple, which had fallen into disrepair, a priest found something that shocked the king and prompted a nationwide spiritual revival. "I have found the Book of the Law in the LORD's Temple!" (2 Chronicles 34:15).

Exactly what the "Book of the Law" was remains a mystery. Most Bible experts guess that the writer was talking about the book of Deuteronomy. It summarizes the Jewish laws reported in Exodus, Leviticus, and Numbers.

Apparently the Jews had lost touch with their laws and had forgotten about their covenant agreement with God. That should come as no surprise because they had just lived through more than half a century of leadership by kings who acted like pagans and worshipped idols—including the nation's most spit-vile king, Manasseh, who sacrificed his own son.

The priest gave the law scroll to a court secretary, who took it to King Josiah. When the king read the contract that his ancestors had made with God, he was horrified. The covenant agreement promised that if the Jews obeyed God he would bless them, but if they disobeyed God he would curse them with disasters, plagues, and invasions.

"Josiah removed all detestable idols from the entire land of Israel and required everyone to worship the LORD their God" (verse 33).

198

Cold Storage: Israel's Most Sacred Relic

Israel's most sacred object, normally kept in the holiest room of the worship center, spent 20 years in a tiny village about 10 miles (16 km) north of Jerusalem. It was the Ark of the Covenant, a gold-covered chest that held the Ten Commandments.

Philistines had captured the Ark of the Covenant in battle and probably had destroyed Israel's worship center at the village of Shiloh as well. They returned their war trophy, however, after it seemed to produce plagues wherever they took it. Apparently without a worship center, the Jews decided to warehouse the ark in the house of a man named Abinadab.

When David became king and established Jerusalem as Israel's capital, he brought the sacred chest to Jerusalem, to a tent worship center they had set up—perhaps a tent much like the one Moses and the Exodus Jews used. "David rose to his feet and said...'It was my desire to build a temple where the Ark of the Lord's Covenant, God's footstool, could rest permanently'" (1 Chronicles 28:2). But that honor would go to his son and successor, Solomon.

Why David called the chest God's footstool is anyone's guess. Some Bible scholars suggest it refers to making a place for God to rest, perhaps since Jews worship God on the Sabbath, a day of rest.

199
Priest Wannabes

A disgruntled worship assistant named Korah incited a rebellion against Moses and Aaron. He argued that he and the other Jews were just as holy as they were and had just as much right to conduct worship rituals as Aaron and his sons, the priests.

Moses pretty much said, "Oh yeah? Let's see what God has to say about that." He told Korah and his 250 followers to do something priestly—report to the worship center with censers. Those were containers that held offerings of burning incense.

When the gang showed up, "the earth opened its mouth and swallowed [the leaders]...Then fire blazed forth from the Lord and burned up the 250 men who were offering incense" (Numbers 16:32,35). A big fire from the Lord, possibly lightning, torched the men and their little fires.

200
Jacob's Fertile Wife

Jacob had a dozen sons by four women—sons whose descendants became the 12 tribes of Israel. Leah delivered six of those sons. "When the Lord saw that Jacob loved Rachel more than Leah, he made it possible for Leah to have children, but not Rachel" (Genesis 29:31 NCV).

The Bible writer didn't say what attracted Jacob to Rachel. But since Jacob was a guy, it's a fair bet that he warmed up to the fact that "Rachel was beautiful and had a good figure" (verse 17 CEV).

Yessiree, that's one bet worth taking.

Leah, on the other hand, had something going on with her eyes. Translators don't quite know what to make of it. Here's a sampling of their guesses...

- "Her eyes didn't sparkle" (CEV).

- "Leah had weak eyes" (NCV).

- "Leah's eyes were lovely" (NRSV).

- "There was no sparkle in Leah's eyes" (NLT).

For all we know, Leah was cross-eyed, bug-eyed, or one-eyed. Whatever her condition, the writer seemed to present it as the flip side of Rachel's coin: "Rachel was beautiful."

But if Leah was nothing else, she was fertile. Leah: six sons. Rachel: two sons.

201
Lebanon's Claim to Fame

What is now the Arab country of Lebanon—a nation currently hostile to Israel—was once an ally of the Jewish people.

King Hiram, who ruled one of Lebanon's city kingdoms along the coast, provided Israel's King Solomon with "cedars from Lebanon" (1 Kings 5:6) for the Jerusalem temple and palace. He also provided artisans to help with the construction and sailors to man Solomon's trade ships.

But if Lebanon exported rot-resistant wood for the temple, it also exported a rotten queen for King Ahab. "He married Jezebel daughter of...the king of Sidon" (1 Kings 16:31 NCV). Jezebel was not a particularly good import. She tried to wipe out the Jewish religion and sub in her own.

- She "tried to kill all the LORD's prophets" (1 Kings 18:4).

- She was likely the reason her husband "built a temple and an altar for Baal" (1 Kings 16:32).

- She supported an entourage of "450 prophets of Baal and the 400 prophets of Asherah" (1 Kings 18:19).

202
Samson Turns Himself In, Temporarily

Samson was thoroughly selfish, as the Bible tells his story. Everything he did seemed driven by selfish desires, especially for sex and revenge. There's just one exception: He turned himself over to the Philistines so they would stop their raids into Jewish cities.

Samson had torched Philistine fields, vineyards, and olive groves. It took several years to replace a vineyard, and a generation to replace an olive grove. Philistines retaliated by invading the Jewish homeland on a manhunt for Samson and by terrorizing Jewish villages.

A group of Jews found Samson and convinced him to surrender. He let them tie him up and deliver him to the Philistines. But as the Philistines were cheering, "he snapped the ropes...Then he found the jawbone of a recently killed donkey. He picked it up and killed 1,000 Philistines with it" (Judges 15:14-15).

Jews renamed the site "Jawbone Hill" (verse 17).

203

Two Non-Jewish Books in the Bible

Jews wrote most of the Bible, with two exceptions: the Gospel of Luke and its sequel, Acts. Both of those books were apparently written by a non-Jew—to a mystery man.

Though both books are written anonymously, early church writers credited Luke, "the beloved doctor" (Colossians 4:14), who remained with Paul to the tragic end. Shortly before Paul's execution in Rome, Paul wrote, "Only Luke is with me" (2 Timothy 4:11).

The unsolved mystery, however, is the identity of Theophilus, the man to whom Luke addressed both letters (Luke 1:1-3; Acts 1:1). Bible experts can only guess who he was.

- A rich Christian who hired Luke to write the story of Jesus and the early church.

- A Roman official Luke was trying to convince that Christianity wasn't a threat to the Empire—perhaps a plea made at Paul's trial.

- A symbolic name to describe all believers. Theophilus means "lover of God."

204

The Lady Who Started the Church in Europe

The first church in Europe met in the home of Lydia, a businesswoman living in Philippi, in what is now northern Greece. "Lydia...sold expensive purple cloth" (Acts 16:14 CEV).

Purple dye came from the Mediterranean Sea, extracted from

the murex snail. That's what made it so expensive. Purple was the top-of-the-line color of cloth in Bible times.

When Paul and his traveling companion, Silas, left what is now Turkey and crossed into what is now Greece, they met Lydia at a Sabbath worship service down by the riverside. Paul told her about Jesus. She became a believer, got baptized, and invited the two men to stay in her home, where "they met with the believers and encouraged them" (verse 40).

Of the many churches Paul planted throughout what is now Syria, Turkey, and Greece, the church at Philippi was the only one on record that he allowed to help support his ministry. "You Philippians were the only ones who gave me financial help when I first brought you the Good News...No other church did this" (Philippians 4:15).

Though Paul collected offerings for others, such as the poor in Jerusalem, he seemed to support himself mainly as a bi-vocational pastor who made and repaired tents (Acts 18:3).

205
Tithe: Resurrecting a Jewish Law

Jewish law required tithing, giving 10 percent of the household income to support the ministry at the Jewish temple.

But the Bible never talks about Christians tithing. That was a Jewish thing. Christians had a more flexible standard: "Make up your own mind what you will give. That will protect you against sob stories and arm-twisting. God loves it when the giver delights in the giving" (2 Corinthians 9:7 MSG).

Church historians say they cannot find a single Christian sermon on tithing until the 1800s. That's when cash-strapped churches in the United States borrowed this particular Jewish law and started using it as a fundraising technique.

Early Christians refused to tithe because they said it was one of the many legalistic Jewish laws that had become "obsolete" (Hebrews 8:13), such as laws about circumcision or eating only kosher food.

American churches, like many churches throughout the world today, were once supported by tax dollars. But in 1833, states started rescinding the religious tax. Churches scrambled for ideas about how to make up the difference. They collected pledges. They took special offerings. They even rented pews. In desperation, they resurrected the old Jewish law about tithing, insisting that it was as relevant and timeless as the Ten Commandments.

Today, tithing remains the top source of income for most churches.

Some church historians have suggested a compromise: Let 10 percent be a good guideline for Christians, but don't sell it as a biblical requirement.

206
Bottom-of-the-Barrel Offerings for God

Malachi, a prophet, was furious about the kinds of good-for-nothing animal offerings Jews were bringing as sacrifices to God.

Jews offered animal sacrifices in remorse for their sins. The death of the animal symbolized the death they deserved for sinning against God.

Jews were not supposed to scrimp on the animals they offered: "You must not offer an animal that is blind, crippled, or injured" (Leviticus 22:22). Yet the prophet Malachi said that was exactly what the Jews were doing—giving Almighty God their leftovers.

"You sacrifice blind animals...You sacrifice disabled or sick animals" (Malachi 1:8 NIRV).

Malachi suggested a test for determining whether the sacrifices were appropriate. "Try giving gifts like that to your governor, and see how pleased he is!" (verse 8).

207

Arab Israel

Not all 12 tribes of Israel settled in what is now Israel. Some moved into what are now the Arab countries of Jordan and Syria. "The tribes of Reuben and Gad with half of the tribe of Manasseh had received their inheritance east of the Jordan River" (Joshua 13:8 GWT). That's now Arab land.

When Moses led the Jews into what is now Jordan and Syria, several tribal leaders liked what they saw. For one, the land was perfect for grazing livestock. For another, the Jews had already conquered the people there.

Kings who had once ruled there had refused to grant safe passage to the Jews as they walked through the land toward what is now Israel. They attacked the Jews, treating them as hostile invaders. So the Jews retaliated and took the land, the animals, and the possessions of the conquered people.

Moses granted the request of these tribal leaders who wanted to settle there. But under one condition—they had to help the other tribes of Israel conquer the land west of the Jordan River, in what is now Israel.

They agreed: "We will cross the Jordan into Canaan fully armed to fight for the LORD, but our property will be here on this side of the Jordan" (Numbers 32:32).

208
Scum Disciple: Not Judas

Before Judas betrayed Jesus, another disciple was probably considered the worst of the bunch because of his former job. "Matthew invited Jesus and his disciples to his home as dinner guests... But when the Pharisees saw this, they asked his disciples, 'Why does your teacher eat with such scum?'" (Matthew 9:10-11).

Jews in Bible times hated tax collectors the way people today hate traitors. That's what Jews considered Bible characters like Matthew and Zacchaeus to be—collaborators with the Roman Empire, which was occupying their homeland.

Romans typically hired locals to serve as tax collectors. That's because locals knew what their neighbors could afford to pay in taxes. Jews bid against one another to work as tax collection subcontractors for the Empire.

Another reason Jews hated Jewish tax collectors is because many tax collectors got greedy. They overcharged people and kept the extra as a bonus.

Some Jewish religious leaders in ancient times said it's perfectly acceptable to tell lies to murderers, robbers, and tax collectors. Others added that a good Jew should never accept change back from a tax collector. It was dirty money. Some added that worship leaders should not even accept charitable contributions from them.

209
The Bible Way to Pick a Preacher

Roll the dice.

That's pretty much how Jesus's disciples replaced Judas. "They cast lots, and Matthias was selected to become an apostle with the other eleven" (Acts 1:26).

It's unclear what exactly the "lots" were. They may have been something as simple as stones marked on one side—as in dark side is heads, light side is tails. In our day, an equivalent might be tossing a coin in the air. Or rolling dice. First pastoral candidate to roll a seven gets the job. "Daddy needs a new pair of shoes."

Jews in ancient times cast lots to make tough decisions because they believed God controlled everything—even the roll of the dice. The Jewish high priest used them, as well, to determine God's will: "Thummin and Urim—the sacred lots…" (Deuteronomy 33:8).

210
King Gone Wild

Babylonian king Nebuchadnezzar is touted as the empire's greatest king and vilified as the ruler who wiped the Jewish nation off the map. He also went insane. "Nebuchadnezzar was driven out of human company, ate grass like an ox, and was soaked in heaven's dew. His hair grew like the feathers of an eagle and his nails like the claws of a hawk" (Daniel 4:33 MSG).

As the Bible tells it, God punished the king for having a big head.

- *Nebuchadnezzar bragged.* "Look at this great city of Babylon! By my own mighty power, I have built this beautiful city as my royal residence to display my majestic splendor" (verse 30).

- *Nebuchadnezzar failed to credit God.* "You will learn this lesson: The Most High God is ruler over every kingdom on earth, and he gives those kingdoms to anyone he chooses" (verse 25 NCV).

It's unclear how long the king remained insane. Fingernails grow about one and a half inches (4 cm) a year, and at one inch (2.5 cm), they start to look like claws.

When he came to his senses, he gave God his due credit, praising and worshipping him.

211

Cheers: A Toast to Jerusalem's New Walls

It may have seemed like someone put a bartender in charge of rebuilding Jerusalem. He was a Jew named Nehemiah, and he led the rebuilding of Jerusalem's walls after Babylonian invaders from what is now Iraq leveled them. He had a radically unrelated job before that: "I was the king's wine taster" (Nehemiah 1:11 NIRV).

As wine steward, Nehemiah tested and served wine to Persian king Artaxerxes about 400 years before Christ. At that time, Persia, in what is now Iran, was the superpower that ruled the Middle East. Persians had defeated the previous superpower, the Iraqi-based Babylonians.

About a century and a half earlier, Babylonians erased the Jewish nation from the political map, leveling all the large cities, including Jerusalem. They took many of the survivors back to what is now Iraq as prisoners. About 50 years later, Persians freed Jewish political prisoners and let them go home and rebuild their cities.

When Nehemiah got word that Jerusalem's walls were still a wreck—after a century of rebuilding—he got bummed. The king noticed his depression and asked what he could do to help (Zoloft wouldn't be invented for another 2400 years). Nehemiah asked for a leave of absence to orchestrate the rebuilding of Jerusalem's walls.

The king not only granted the request but also gave him an armed escort and a letter directing the regional governors to give him lumber for the construction.

Jews restored the walls in a mere 52 days (Nehemiah 6:15)—perhaps a quick patch job that would hold until they could finish a more permanent wall.

212

Utilities in Heaven: Lights

In the last book in the Bible, Revelation, the writer says he saw a vision of heaven—golden streets, gemstone walls, and a river down Main Street. He said heaven is well lit. "The city has no need of sun or moon, for the glory of God illuminates the city, and the Lamb is its light" (Revelation 21:23).

Evidently, God and other celestial beings glow. That's often how Bible writers describe them.

- *Burning bush.* God appeared to Moses as a bush "engulfed in flames" (Exodus 3:2).

- *Fire on the mountain.* When God appeared to Moses on Mount Sinai, he "descended on it in the form of fire" (Exodus 19:18).

- *Jesus, in glowing terms.* In a Bible event called the Trans-figuration—from the Greek word *metamorphoo*, from which we get *metamorphosis*—Jesus "was transfigured" in front of three of his disciples. "His face shone like the sun, and his clothes became as white as the light" (Matthew 17:2-3 TNIV).

213
The World's Longest River

The Nile is the longest river in the world—long enough to stretch from New York City to Los Angeles and most of the way back again. Nearly twice as long as the Mississippi River, the Nile stretches more than 4000 miles (about 6600 km).

It starts in the tiny nation of Burundi in the Great Lakes region of central Africa. Flowing north, it cuts a fertile path through ten nations before emptying into the Mediterranean Sea along the north shores of Egypt.

Without the Nile, Egypt would be a vacant desert. But because of it, Egyptians in Bible times enjoyed a drought-resistant life alongside the banks of a reliable source of water.

Most Egyptians—then and now—live along the banks of the Nile on a ten-mile-wide (16 km) strip of green earth that snakes through the desert.

214

Noah's Ark and the Cleveland Browns

You could park two of Noah's arks side by side on a football field, but you'd need both end zones, and you wouldn't want to pay the parking fee. "Make the boat 450 feet long [137 m], 75 feet wide [23 m], and 45 feet high [14 m]" (Genesis 6:15).

A cruise ship would dwarf the ark, the boat Noah used to save his family and a boatload of animals from the flood. Typical cruise ships are about twice as long as Noah's boat, and they carry between 2000 and 3000 passengers.

Surprisingly, though, the storage space inside Noah's boat was equal to the space in about 370 railroad boxcars. Not enough for all the animals in the world, many Bible experts say, but certainly enough for animals in the region if the flood was localized to the place where civilization began—the Euphrates River Valley, in what is now Iraq.

Parked on a football field, the ark would stretch all the way across the 100-yard (91 m) playing field, extending through both 10-yard (9 m) end zones, and pushing another 15 yards (14 m) into the stands on each end of the field. But the ark was only about half as wide as the playing field, so Noah could have parked two boats side by side.

The roof of the ark would rise more than twice the height of the goalposts, which stand 20 feet (6 m) high, with the crossbar situated halfway up the posts.

215

Dwindling Lifespans

The lifespan of humans was measured in centuries until the flood. "Methuselah [Noah's grandfather] lived 969 years, and then he died" (Genesis 5:27). After the flood, lifespans dropped to about what we experience today. "Moses was 120 years old when he died" (Deuteronomy 34:7).

The Bible isn't the only ancient source that says people before the great flood lived for centuries. A 4000-year-old clay prism from Sumeria (in what is now Iraq), the world's first-known civilization, reports that there were only eight kings up until the great flood—and that those kings ruled for total of 241,200 years. That's an average of 30,000 years per king. The shortest reign reported was 18,600 years.

Those numbers make the Bible's oldest character, nearly 1000-year-old Methuselah, look like he died in diapers. As the Bible reports it, lifespans dwindled after the flood.

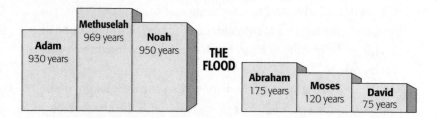

Some Bible experts speculate that the high numbers were polite exaggerations, a way of honoring revered ancestors. Other students of the Bible say the numbers may be accurate and that the flood somehow drastically cut lifespans—perhaps by releasing underground toxins or turning constant cloud cover into blue skies, exposing everyone to harmful radiation.

216

A Bed for a Giant

Jews of the Exodus conquered the nation ruled by King Og, a giant. They displayed his huge bed, which measured 13 feet long by 6 feet wide (4 m by 1.8 m) as a war trophy. "You can still see it on display in Rabbah" (Deuteronomy 3:11 MSG).

Og ruled a kingdom of 60 villages—each one protected by huge walls—scattered throughout modern-day Syria and Jordan. He's a perfect example of why first-generation Jews on their exodus out of Egypt refused to invade the Promised Land. They were frightened off by the scouting reports about walled cities and giants. Second-generation Jews, however, trusted that God would give them the land.

When they asked permission to pass peacefully through the Arab territory east of the Jordan River, Arab kings mobilized their armies and attacked the Jews. Bad decision.

Jews won the war, captured the land, and treated it as part of God's package deal—East Bank of the Promised Land. Some of the Jews—the tribes of Gad, Reuben, and half the tribe of Manasseh—liked the land so much, they decided to live there.

217

How to Stop a Jewish Attack

When the Jews attacked the forces of King Mesha in Moab, in what is now part of the Arab country of Jordan, Mesha chose a horrifying strategy to drive off the Jews. "The king of Moab got his oldest son. He was the son who would become the next king after him. He offered his son as a sacrifice on the city wall" (2 Kings 3:27 NIRV).

In many Bible stories of Old Testament times, Israel was forced to pay taxes to some superpower, such as the Iraqi-based Assyrians or Babylonians. But sometimes, the Jews forced their weaker neighbors to pay annual taxes. King Mesha was one such neighbor. He apparently decided that his army was strong enough to break free from Israel.

He was wrong. Jews came to collect. War broke out.

Jews destroyed towns throughout the kingdom of Moab. They cornered King Mesha and his remaining men in the only surviving fortified city. That's when King Mesha sacrificed his oldest son, the crown prince.

"That shocked and terrified the men of Israel. So they pulled back. And they returned to their own land" (verse 27 NIRV).

In an ancient report called the Moabite Stone, chiseled in black rock, King Mesha tells his story of breaking free from Israel's long oppression. It's one instance in which archaeology reinforces the Bible's account of what happened.

218
Stiff Penalty for Early Withdrawal

As Jewish law dictated, Onan married his brother's widow. But instead of providing her with heirs to take care of her in her old age, as Jewish law said he should do, when he had sex with her he refused to release his semen inside her. The Bible writer tells us, "The LORD considered it evil for Onan to deny a child to his dead brother. So the LORD took Onan's life" (Genesis 38:10).

It seems like an odd law to us today, requiring a dead man's closest relative to marry the widow. But it was an ancient form of social security, to provide for the woman. When parents got old, their kids took care of them.

But this widow, Tamar, had no children. No one to take care of her in her old age. No one to inherit her husband's land and other assets—no one except Onan, whom the Bible writer says God killed.

Some Bible scholars say the writer was speculating about Onan's death, drawing the conclusion that God must have caused it because God is LORD of all and nothing happens without his consent.

In a disturbing twist to the story, after Onan died, Tamar disguised herself as a prostitute and managed to get herself pregnant by her father-in-law, Judah. She had twin boys who, by Jewish law, could have called their father Grandpa.

219
Paul's Oddball Version of an Underground Railroad

Paul converted a runaway slave named Onesimus—and promptly told the slave to go back to his master. In a letter he gave Onesimus to take to the slave master, he wrote, "I am sending him back to you. This is like sending you a part of myself…Maybe Onesimus was gone for a while so that you could have him back forever—no longer as a slave but better than a slave—as a dear brother" (Philemon 12,15-16 GWT).

Instead of bucking the system and the prevailing law of Roman times, which allowed slavery, Paul worked inside the system. As the law required, he sent the runaway slave home—but with an incredibly powerful letter, arm-twisting the Christian slave owner, Philemon, to free Onesimus and send him back to help Paul.

"I wanted to keep him here with me. Then he could have served me in your place while I am in prison for spreading the Good News. Yet, I didn't want to do anything without your consent" (Philemon 1:13-14 GWT).

In other words, "Give me your permission."

Some scholars say that it looks like the letter worked. About 50 years after Paul wrote this letter, a church leader named Ignatius wrote a letter to the church leader at Ephesus—Bishop Onesimus.

220

Solomon's Mysterious Fleet of Ships

King Solomon had a fleet of ships that sailed on the Red Sea, wedged between Africa on the west side and what are now Saudi Arabia and other Arab countries in the east. "They sailed to Ophir and brought back to Solomon some sixteen tons [fourteen metric tons] of gold…they also brought rich cargoes of red sandalwood and precious jewels" (1 Kings 9:28; 10:11).

The big question is, where was Ophir?

Solomon's trading venture was actually a joint project with King Hiram, from what is now Lebanon. Hiram's kingdom on the Mediterranean coast was famous for its fleet of merchant ships. Solomon and Hiram teamed up to trade some of their natural resources with a kingdom somewhere south.

Some of the trade items they brought back—especially the gold and rare wood—sound like they may have come from East Africa. But some Bible scholars speculate Solomon's ships may have sailed as far away as South Africa or even India.

221

Jewish Palestinians

The word Palestine comes from the name of the Philistines—a race of people in Bible times that didn't like the Jews very much. "The Philistines invaded Judah" (Judges 15:9 CEV).

These first Palestinians were not Arabs. They were more likely Greeks, or at least neighbors of Greeks. Historians sometimes call them the Seafarers, a warlike people from somewhere in the Mediterranean—perhaps islands off of Greece. They settled on what is now the coast of Israel and the Palestinian Authority.

In our English Bibles, the homeland of the Philistines is often described as "Philistia." But in the original Hebrew, writers called it the land of the *Pelistim*, meaning "Philistines."

In Greek, the language in which the New Testament was written, the word is *Palastium*. Romans adapted this to Latin, calling it *Palaestine*. They eventually gave that name to the entire Jewish homeland, perhaps to dis the Jews for their repeated revolts. Instead of the Jewish-friendly name of Judea, the land became known as Palestine.

That name is all that's left of the Philistines. Their people and their culture were assimilated into other Middle Eastern kingdoms, probably including the Jewish nation. If so, some Jews have Palestinian blood in their veins and vice versa.

222

Paul 1, Sorcerer 0

Sergius Paulus, governor of the island of Cyprus, was the first Roman official on record to convert to Christianity.

When Paul and Barnabas were telling him the story of Jesus, a local sorcerer "interfered and urged the governor to pay no attention…He was trying to keep the governor from believing" (Acts 13:8). Sadly for him, his interference had the opposite effect.

Paul called the sorcerer the "son of the devil, full of every sort of deceit and fraud, enemy of all that is good!" (verse 10). It gets worse. Paul announced the consequence of his interference: "The Lord is going to punish you by making you completely blind for a while" (Acts 13:11 CEV). Sure enough, "instantly mist and darkness came over the man's eyes, and he began groping around begging for someone to take his hand and lead him. When the governor saw what happened, he became a believer" (verses 11-12).

223

The Bible Ends Here

A man named John said he wrote Revelation, the last book of the Bible, in exile. "I was exiled to the island of Patmos for preaching the word of God" (Revelation 1:9).

Romans banished people for a variety of reasons, including for teaching outlawed religions. By the time Revelation was written, near the end of the first century, Christianity qualified.

Some Bible scholars say they doubt that the John of Revelation was the apostle John, partly because Revelation's John mentions "the twelve apostles of the Lamb" (Revelation 21:14) but doesn't identify himself as one of those twelve.

Patmos may have been one of the Roman Empire's penal colonies. It was a tiny island about 10 miles (16 km) long and 6 miles (10 km) wide. It rested about 40 miles (64 km) off the west coast Turkey.

224
One Tough Preacher

In the apostle Paul's 30 years of ministry on the road, he suffered a lot of physical abuse and dangerous situations. "Five different times the Jewish leaders gave me thirty-nine lashes. Three times I was beaten with rods. Once I was stoned. Three times I was shipwrecked. Once I spent a whole night and a day adrift at sea" (2 Corinthians 11:24-25).

Paul was also imprisoned at least five times—probably more. Some Bible experts estimate that Paul may have spent about half of his 30-year ministry in prison. When he was out of prison and on the road preaching, he faced persecution from three groups.

- Jews who hated his "blasphemous" preaching that Jesus was the Messiah and the Son of God.

- Jewish Christians who hated his teaching that non-Jews could skip the Jewish laws, including laws requiring circumcision and a kosher diet.

- Folks of other religions who felt threatened by his preaching because so many left those religions and converted to Christianity.

Paul, the Very Jewish Roman

The apostle Paul, a Jew, was also a Roman citizen.

Arrested in Jerusalem for causing a riot at the temple, Paul avoided a lashing by invoking his citizenship rights. He asked the Roman officer in charge, "Is it legal for you to whip a Roman citizen who hasn't even been tried?" (Acts 22:25). The officer told his commander what Paul had said.

> So the commander went over and asked Paul, "Are you a Roman citizen?"
>
> "Yes, I certainly am," Paul replied.
>
> "I am, too," the commander muttered, "and it cost me plenty!"
>
> Paul answered, "But I am a citizen by birth!" (verses 27-28).

Bible writers don't tell the backstory about why Paul was a citizen by birth. But Roman historians do. Several decades before Paul was born, Romans invaded his home region in what is now southern Turkey. Instead of resisting the invaders, the people of Paul's hometown, Tarsus, welcomed them warmly.

As a reward for their hospitality, the commander, Mark Antony, declared the people free Roman citizens in 42 BC. That gave them rights people in conquered nations did not have, such as the right to a trial and to a quick death instead of crucifixion if they were convicted of capital offense. They also benefited from some nice tax breaks.

226
A Thorn in Paul's Side

Paul had a problem—and an odd way of looking at it. "To keep me from becoming proud, I was given a thorn in my flesh, a messenger from Satan to torment me and keep me from becoming proud" (2 Corinthians 12:7).

He never bothered to say what that thorn in his flesh was. But whatever it was, it apparently kept him humble. Many Bible experts guess he was talking about an embarrassing physical problem. Here are two guesses.

- *Recurring malaria.* Paul traveled through some swampy lands in what is now southern Turkey.

- *Poor eyesight.* Paul dictated many of his letters, once adding this note with his signature: "Notice what large letters I use as I write these closing words in my own handwriting" (Galatians 6:11).

Other Bible experts suggest he may have had some embarrassing relational problems, such as the troublesome church he started in Corinth. The Greek word translated *thorn* doesn't show up anywhere else in the New Testament, but it is in the Bible Paul used, the Greek translation of the Old Testament. There it describes what the troublesome Canaanites would become to the Jews: "splinters in your eyes and thorns in your sides" (Numbers 33:55).

227

Peter's Awkward Nickname

Jesus seemed to know ahead of time that his top disciple, Simon, would wimp out on the night Jesus was arrested, denying three times that he even knew Jesus. So the nickname Jesus gave him could sound like a joke. "'From now on your name is Cephas' (or Peter, which means 'Rock')" (John 1:42 MSG).

It's odd enough that the first thing out of Jesus's mouth when he met Peter wasn't a greeting, like "Hello. Nice to meet you." Instead, after "looking intently at Simon," the first thing Jesus said was, "Your name is Simon, son of John—but you will be called Cephas" (verse 42).

That's not what most folks would call a normal greeting.

Cephas means "rock" in Aramaic, the language most Jews spoke. Their ancestors picked it up during their exile a few centuries earlier in what is now Iraq. *Peter* is "rock" in Greek, the international language of the day, the language in which the New Testament was written.

In Bible times, kings, rabbis, and other people in authority sometimes gave new names to people under them. In some cases, it was a way for leaders to send the message that they were the boss. But Jesus seemed to be giving Peter a name that would describe his destiny.

That name certainly does not describe the future for which Peter is best known—denying that he knew Jesus after Jesus was arrested. But that name does describe what Peter became before and after the crucifixion of Jesus. Peter led the disciples as their chief spokesman. Whenever we read a list of the disciples in the Bible, Peter's name appears first.

After the crucifixion, Peter led the Christian movement, preaching the sermon that convinced more than 3000 Jews to become followers of Jesus.

228

What Was Paul Thinking?

In one of the apostle Paul's weirdest and most vexing comments, he said, "Women will be saved through childbearing, assuming they continue to live in faith, love, holiness, and modesty" (1 Timothy 2:15).

Well, that sounds like rotten luck for infertile couples. Or for couples who simply decided they didn't want to have kids.

Bible experts fire off a cartridge full of theories, trying to hit on Paul's point—enough theories that it looks like they're shooting in the dark. Most scholars seem to agree Paul was not saying what it sounds like he was saying—that women have to produce children if they want to make it into heaven. After all, Paul said in a previous letter, "God saved you by his grace when you believed" (Ephesians 2:8).

Some Bible experts guess Paul wrote that as a way to push back at the wrongheaded preachers who taught that celibacy was better than marriage. Others say they wonder if he was reacting to women who became so involved in church work that their families suffered. If that is so, Paul was assuring women they didn't need to do anything more than live out their faith by accepting their God-given role as wife and mother.

229

Crossing the Red Sea Without a Boat

Or did they cross on a bike? That's a question Bible experts would love to ask Moses.

When Moses led the Jewish refugees out of Egypt, God parted a body of water for the Jews and then released the water to drown the Egyptian army that was chasing them. The Bible writer says, "The LORD...threw the chariots and army of Egypt's king into the Red Sea" (Exodus 15:3-4 CEV).

In Hebrew, the original language of the Old Testament, the body of water was simply called *yam sup*. *Yam* means "sea." *Sup* means "reeds" or sometimes "far away." For that reason, many Bible experts say the translators were a tad presumptuous in identifying this body of water with the Red Sea. They say a more literal translation would be "a sea of reeds," or perhaps "a faraway sea."

Some Bible scholars speculate that the body of water God parted was actually one of the reed-laced lakes the Jews would have had to walk past before they got to the Red Sea—possibly Lake Timseh (aka Crocodile Lake), Great Bitter Lake, or Little Bitter Lake.

230

How to Part the Sea

To part the sea for Moses and the Exodus Jews who were trapped between the water and the Egyptian army, "the LORD opened up a path through the water with a strong east wind. The wind blew all that night, turning the seabed into dry land" (Exodus 14:21).

Scientists who specialize in meteorology and oceanography

have actually studied whether a strong wind could part the Gulf of Suez, the narrow finger of water in the northern tip of the Red Sea. In separate studies, scientists concluded that a strong, sustained eastern wind could in fact push back the water, mimicking the effect of low tide. This could extend the beach by as much as a mile (1.6 km).*

Once the wind stopped, scientists say, the water would rush back into place—up to 10 feet (3 m) deep—within 30 minutes.

Some say this may have been what happened to Napoleon when he invaded Egypt in 1799 as he rode along the Red Sea shoreline. Receded water rushed back to shore, knocking him off his horse and nearly drowning him.

231
Mysterious City of Seven Hills

Writing in Revelation about end-time visions he experienced, John said he saw a prostitute riding a beast with seven heads and that the heads represented "the seven hills where the woman rules" (Revelation 17:9).

Most Bible scholars say John was hinting at the city of Rome. "Anyone with wisdom can figure this out. The seven heads that the woman is sitting on stand for seven hills. These heads are also seven kings. Five of the kings are dead. One is ruling now, and the other one has not yet come. But when he does, he will rule for only a little while" (Revelation 17:9-10 CEV).

According to an ancient Roman tradition, before Rome was a city, it was seven individual settlements on separate, neighboring

---

* The separate scientific studies were reported in the *Bulletin of the Russian Academy of Sciences*, 2004, and the *Bulletin of the American Meteorological Society*, March 1992.

hills. Excavations suggest people lived on those hills as early as 1000 BC—the time of King David. Legend says the settlements united and built a wall around all seven hills to become the city of Rome.

In one theory about John's reference to the seven kings, he was talking about Roman emperors who ruled from about the time of Jesus's birth.

1. Augustus (ruled 27 BC–AD 14)
2. Tiberius (AD 14–37)
3. Caligula (AD 37–41)
4. Claudius (AD 41–54)
5. Nero (AD 54–68)
6. Vespasian (AD 69–79)
7. Titus (the short-term emperor John mentioned) (AD 79–81)

All of these emperors likely reigned before John wrote Revelation, many scholars say. These scholars put the date of Revelation somewhere in the AD 90s.

232

Date with an Energizing Prostitute

Philistines in the city of Gaza lay in waiting to jump Samson after he came out of a prostitute's house. They figured he'd be exhausted and vulnerable. They were wrong.

> Samson was in bed with the woman until midnight. Then he got up, seized the doors of the city gate and the

two gateposts, bolts and all, hefted them on his shoulder, and carried them to the top of the hill that faces Hebron (Judges 16:3 MSG).

Samson had been terrorizing the Philistine countryside along the Mediterranean coast of what are now Israel and the Gaza Strip. Retaliating for their execution of his wife and father-in-law, he tied torches to the tails of 300 foxes and "let the foxes run through the grain fields of the Philistines. He burned all their grain to the ground…He also destroyed their vineyards and olive groves" (Judges 15:5).

That was a big deal. In Bible times it took newly planted grapevines three to five years to produce their first full crop. Olive trees took even longer—40 or 50 years before they were most productive. So when the Philistines saw him go into the house of a prostitute in Gaza, they figured they could jump him when he came outside the next morning, exhausted from a sleepless night of partying. Payback time for what he had done to them.

But he was quite finished with the lady by around midnight and energized enough to carry the massive town gates nearly all the way from Gaza to Hebron, a stretch of about 40 miles (64 km).

233
King of the Donkey Herders

Like many young men in Israel, Saul worked with his father tending the herds of donkeys and perhaps other livestock as well. But if hints in the Bible are correct, Saul had a special fondness for donkeys. "Kish owned some donkeys, but they had run off. So he told Saul [his son]…'Go look for the donkeys'" (1 Samuel 9:3 CEV).

And Saul evidently preferred herding donkeys to ruling people. When the prophet Samuel brought the tribal leaders together to introduce them to their first king, Saul was "hiding behind the baggage" (1 Samuel 10:22 CEV). And perhaps by the animals that usually carried the baggage—donkeys.

234
Wise Solomon's Dumb Side

One Bible writer described King Solomon as the wisest man who ever lived or would ever live. Yet Solomon did a couple of really dumb things, ignoring Jewish laws forbidding polygamy and idolatry. "Seven hundred of his wives were daughters of kings, but he also married three hundred other women. As Solomon got older, some of his wives led him to worship their gods" (1 Kings 11:3-4 CEV).

It was customary in the ancient Middle East for powerful men to entertain a large harem of wives. The size of the harem reflected the measure of the man. With 1000 wives, Solomon would have been perceived as quite the man.

But Jewish law clearly said, "The king must not take many wives for himself, because they will turn his heart away from the LORD" (Deuteronomy 17:17). This warning Moses gave when he delivered God's law to the people is exactly what happened to Solomon.

As a result of Solomon's sin, God told him, "I'm going to take your kingdom from you and give it to one of your officials" (1 Kings 11:11 CEV). Sure enough, when Solomon's son became king, the nation split in two. The northern tribes became the Jewish nation of Israel. The southern tribes became the Jewish nation of Judah.

235

Solomon's Prefab Temple

Jerusalem's first temple was essentially a prefab building pieced together like giant stone Legos.

Silence was apparently one of the building codes that King Solomon instituted. "Solomon did not want the noise of hammers and axes to be heard at the place where the temple was being built. So he had the workers shape the blocks of stone at the quarry" (1 Kings 6:7 CEV).

Bible experts say this was probably out of respect for the sacred site. Jews had been worshipping on this Jerusalem hilltop for decades—ever since Solomon's father, King David, bought the former bedrock threshing field from a farmer and built an altar there.

Solomon's white limestone temple followed a rectangular floor plan and stood some 90 feet (27 m) long, 30 feet (9 m) wide, and 45 feet (14 m) high.

It lasted for about 400 years. In 586 BC, Babylonian invaders from what is now Iraq stripped away all the temple's gold and leveled the sacred building along with the rest of Jerusalem.

236

Paul's Last Request

The apostle Paul, on the brink of his execution, wrote a letter to his dear friend Timothy, who was pastoring a church near what is now the west coast of Turkey. "Timothy, please come as soon as you can...Be sure to bring the coat I left with Carpus at Troas. Also bring my books, and especially my papers" (2 Timothy 4:9,13).

It's a deeply personal, heartbreaking letter to read—a tender letter that Paul may never have intended anyone to read but Timothy, a colleague he called "my dear son" (2 Timothy 1:2). "My life is coming to an end," he wrote from a prison in Rome. "It is now time for me to be poured out as a sacrifice to God. I have fought the good fight. I have completed the race. I have kept the faith" (2 Timothy 4:6-7 GWT).

Like many people about to die, Paul didn't want to die alone. He wanted the people he loved most to be with him. Timothy qualified.

Paul had assigned him to pastor the growing church in Ephesus, some 1000 miles (1600 km) east of Rome. No one seems to know if Timothy rushed to Paul or if he got there in time. Traveling mostly by land, it would have taken Timothy a month or two to reach Paul. By sea, with favorable winds, he could have made the trip in about two weeks.

237
When to Put a Trophy Wife on the Shelf

Drunken King Xerxes summoned his drop-dead gorgeous wife, Queen Vashti, to make an appearance at his all-guy drinking party. When she refused, Xerxes announced, "Vashti is permanently banned from King Xerxes' presence" (Esther 1:19 MSG).

Demoting the queen to just another wife in the harem isn't the only thing the Persian king did. He also decided to use his wife's stubborn refusal as an opportunity to teach a lesson to every woman in his empire. "He sent bulletins to every part of the kingdom, to each province in its own script, to each people in their own language: 'Every man is master of his own house; whatever he says, goes'" (verse 22 MSG).

So there. Drop that in your pot and cook it, lady.

Xerxes picked his next queen in the most manly fashion of all.

He held a beauty contest and married the winner, a Jewish orphan named Esther.

<h1 style="text-align:center">238</h1>

Moses Gets Quarter Pounders to Go

When the Exodus Jews complained that they were hungry for meat, "the LORD sent a wind that brought quail from the sea and let them fall all around the camp. For miles in every direction there were quail flying about three feet above the ground" (Numbers 11:31).

Many other Bible translations say the quail were stacked three feet (92 cm) high on the ground. But if ancient Egyptian pictures are any indication, it is just as likely that they were flying at that hedge-height altitude—lumbering low and slow against the wind on their long-distance migration.

The quail were probably the stubby little birds with the repeating name *Coturnix coturnix*. They weigh in at about a quarter of a pound (113 g) and stretch half the length of a foot-long hotdog (15 cm).

Ancient pictures show Egyptians catching birds with their bare hands. That may be how the Jews pulled them from the air too. Many of the birds may have collapsed on the ground, unable to fly to save their lives—a bit like some runners drop to the ground after giving their all in a race.

239
Don't Dis God's Stuff

The Bible says God struck a man dead while the gent was transporting Israel's most sacred object to Jerusalem. It was the Ark of the Covenant, a gold-covered chest that held the Ten Commandments. "Uzzah reached out his hand and steadied the Ark of God. Then the LORD's anger was aroused against Uzzah, and God struck him dead because of this" (2 Samuel 6:6-7).

The big question is, why would God kill someone for simply trying to protect the Ark of the Covenant? Bible experts are left guessing.

- The only ones allowed to touch the Ark of the Covenant were priests who were ritually clean. Uzzah was neither a priest nor ritually clean. He should not have touched the sacred object for any reason.

- Uzzah and his brother transported the Ark in an oxcart. Priests were supposed to carry it.

- Uzzah died of natural causes, but the Bible writer simply presumed God killed him because God controls everything.

King David managed to get the Ark to Jerusalem in a second, more respectful attempt three months later.

240

God Decides to Kill Moses?

In a strange sidebar of a story, the Exodus writer said God nearly killed either Moses or his son—it's not clear which—while Moses and his family were on their way to Egypt so Moses could free the Jews. To stop God from the killing, "Moses' wife, Zipporah, took a flint knife and circumcised her son" (Exodus 4:25).

Perhaps the best guess about what was going on is that Moses was destined to become Israel's great lawgiver, yet he had failed to observe the single most basic law God had given to Abraham, the father of the Jews. "Circumcise every baby boy...Any male who is not circumcised will be cut off from his people, because he has broken my agreement" (Genesis 17:13-14 NCV).

In fairness to Moses, he had spent the first 40 years of his life as a prince in Egypt. He spent the second 40 years of his life as a shepherd in exile east of Egypt, along Jordan's southern border with Saudi Arabia.

Still, he and his wife apparently knew of the custom, which would explain why Zipporah circumcised her son.

241

Leading Chicago Through the Desert

The Bible says Moses led quite a group out of slavery in Egypt. "There were about 600,000 men, plus all the women and children" (Exodus 12:37).

Add one woman for each man and two children for each couple, and you end up with the population of Chicago—some 2.4 million souls wandering through the Sinai desert for about 40 years.

Many students of the Bible take those numbers literally, saying that the God of creation could sustain that many people even in the Martian-like badlands of the Sinai Peninsula. Others take the numbers symbolically. Hebrew letters had numerical equivalents, a bit like A = 1, B = 2.

A later census reported the exact number: 603,550. If we add Moses to the census, we get the number 603,551. That's the total we get when we add the number equivalents to the common Hebrew phrase used to identify the Jews—"sons of Israel." With that in mind, some argue that the body count was simply a way of saying that all the "sons of Israel" were there, however many there were.

242
PETA Would Not Approve

God was the first one on record to kill an animal, according to the writer of Genesis, the first book in the Bible. "The LORD God made clothes out of animal skins for Adam and his wife to wear" (Genesis 3:21 NIRV).

Since the world's first sin, animals have been paying the price for humanity's trangressions. Shortly after the Exodus, God set up a sacrificial system that allowed Jews to kill animals as substitutes for the death sentence people deserved for sinning. As Moses explained to the Jews, quoting God, "The life of each creature is in its blood. So I have given you the blood of animals to pay for your sin on the altar" (Leviticus 17:11 NIRV). The bloody ritual served as a perpetual reminder that sin is deadly serious.

Just as it was for the animals God killed to cover Adam and Eve's sin.

243

Moses Down Under

God told Moses not to climb steps up to the altar when making sacrifices. "If you do, someone might see your naked body under your robes" (Exodus 20:26 NIRV).

Before Jews on their Exodus out of slavery in Egypt built a tent worship center known as the tabernacle, they apparently burned their sacrificial animals the old-fashioned way—on top of a pile of dirt or stones.

That's probably the kind of altar God had in mind, scholars say, when he told Moses not to climb steps to the top. Some ancient Canaanite altars in what is now Israel included steps to the top. One stone altar in Megiddo, a fort-city in the Carmel Mountains in what is now northern Israel, had steps five feet (1.5 m) high. They led up to a round platform about 26 feet (8 m) across.

When Jews later built their portable worship center, they added a square altar about 7½ feet square and 4½ feet high (2.3 x 1.4 m). They framed it in wood, covered it with bronze, and topped it with bronze grating—a bit like we would find on a barbecue grill. That's where they burned the meat they sacrificed to God to atone for their sins.

When priests climbed the steps to that altar, they wore "linen undergarments" (Leviticus 6:10).

244
Keeping It Kosher on the Dinner Table

The Jews were allowed to eat some strange critters. "The insects you are permitted to eat include all kinds of locusts, bald locusts, crickets, and grasshoppers" (Leviticus 11:22).

It could sound like God was playing a joke on the Jews. Today's special: crispy locust salad, cricket soup, all the fried grasshoppers you can eat. Off the menu: buttered lobster, soft-shell crabs, and shrimp. Reserved for non-Jews.

Scholars in various fields have tried to make sense of the kosher menu that Moses said God gave the Jews. Theories include...

- The permitted food was healthier.

- It was more normal (fish without scales isn't normal, so catfish was forbidden).

- It was simply God teaching the Jews to obey, a bit like an Army sergeant ordering new recruits to dig a hole and then fill it back in.

Early Christians taught that Jesus initiated a new covenant agreement between God and humanity, making the old covenant laws obsolete (Hebrews 8:13).

Jesus offered his take on the status of the expiring kosher food laws: "It's not what goes into your mouth that defiles you; you are defiled by the words that come out of your mouth" (Matthew 15:11).

245

No Promised Land for Moses

Moses performed one miracle in a way that somehow displeased God, so the LORD decided that Moses would not step foot on the Promised Land, now called Israel.

> Moses raised his hand and struck the rock twice with the staff, and water gushed out...But the LORD said to Moses and Aaron, "Because you did not trust me enough to demonstrate my holiness to the people of Israel, you will not lead them into the land I am giving them!" (Numbers 20:11-12).

Unfortunately for curious souls, the Bible writer doesn't say what Moses and his older brother Aaron did wrong. That leaves Bible experts guessing...

- *Disobedience.* God told Moses simply to speak to the rock, but Moses struck the rock twice.

- *Taking credit for the miracle.* Moses angrily shouted to the Jews, "Must we bring you water from this rock?" (Numbers 20:10).

- *Temper tantrum.* "Moses exploded and lost his temper" (Psalm 106:33 MSG).

- *If you can't say something good...* Out of respect for Moses, the writer chose not to say anything about the sin.

246

The Walls Came Tumblin' Down

Jericho was the first city Joshua and the Jews attacked when they invaded what is now Israel. They used an unconventional technique to breach the massive, heavily fortified city wall.

"Priests blew the trumpets. As soon as the fighting men heard the sound, they gave a loud shout. Then the wall fell down" (Joshua 6:20 NIRV).

Most Christians read this story as a supernatural miracle from God. Other Christians wonder if it was more a miracle of timing than of God striking the walls with supernatural force. They wonder if an earthquake brought the walls down.

Jericho sits in the Jordan River Valley, directly above a seam in the earth's crust. The Bible says that earlier, the Jordan River had stopped flowing to allow them to cross during springtime flooding. Earthquakes have dropped clay cliffs into the Jordan, damming it up many times—once at the very place where the Bible says the water stopped for Joshua and the Jews (see number 110, "How to Stop a River").

Some Christians aware of this geographical history say they wonder if the earthquake and its aftershocks brought down the walls of Jericho.

247
Shady Ladies in Jesus's Family Tree

The Gospel of Matthew includes four women in Jesus's family tree—which is pretty unusual for any genealogy written in Bible times, when men ruled the roost and women were treated as property. But what's even more unusual is that these four women were of questionable repute—Tamar, Rahab, Bathsheba, and Ruth (Matthew 1:3,5-6).

It's a mystery why Matthew picked the rotten apples from Jesus's family tree and left the good apples hanging. He skipped the headliners, like Abraham's wife, Sarah, and went directly to prostitutes and other ladies who seemed to need their scruples tightened:

- Tamar, a widow who disguised herself as a prostitute and seduced her father-in-law. She had twins by him.

- Rahab, the Jericho prostitute who helped Joshua and the Jews invade her homeland.

- Ruth, a widow who took a bath, smothered herself in perfume, and then snuck under the covers of the man she wanted to marry.

- Bathsheba, a married woman who got pregnant by the very married King David.

Some Bible experts say they wonder if Matthew chose those women because he was about to tell the story of Mary, an unmarried gal who became pregnant by the Holy Spirit. Perhaps Matthew wanted to silence Jews who would criticize Mary as a sex sinner.

Another theory is that Matthew was simply trying to show that God sometimes works out his plan through the most unlikely of souls.

248
Queen of Shopping

Sheba's queen visited King Solomon, the Bible says, to see if he was as smart as she had heard. Bible experts say the story suggests an ulterior motive—a shopping spree. "She gave the king a gift of 9,000 pounds [4,000 kg] of gold, great quantities of spices, and precious jewels…King Solomon gave the queen of Sheba whatever she asked for" (1 Kings 10:10,13).

It's a mystery where the kingdom of Sheba was. The most popular guess of the moment is Yemen, an Arab country on the southwest tip of the Arabian Peninsula, beside the Red Sea.

Solomon built a fleet of trading ships to sail the Red Sea, exporting Israel's products—such as olive oil and wine—while importing lots of extravagant products. "Once every three years the ships returned, loaded with gold, silver, ivory, apes, and peacocks" (verse 22).

Some scholars say the Bible writer used the story about the queen of Sheba shopping in Jerusalem to introduce Solomon's trading ventures—as though saying people "came to consult him" was a polite way of saying they came to do business. "People from every nation came to consult him and to hear the wisdom God had given him. Year after year everyone who visited brought him gifts of silver and gold, clothing, weapons, spices, horses, and mules" (1 Kings 10:24-25).

Like the queen of Sheba, they likely didn't go home empty-handed.

249

No-Good Northerners

In 420 years of Jewish history—from the time of their first king to their last—Jews lived under the reign of 42 rulers. Only half a dozen get a Bible thumbs-up as godly kings: David, Solomon, Asa, Jehoshaphat, Hezekiah, and Josiah.* (Uzziah and Jotham get honorable mention.†)

It's odd enough that only six Jewish kings deserve a smiley face sticker beside their name on a Sunday school chart. What's even more surprising is that not one of them ruled the northern Jewish nation of Israel. All six of the good guys lived in the south.

David and Solomon ruled in Jerusalem while Israel was still a single nation. The other four ruled in Jerusalem after Israel split in two, with Judah as the southern Jewish nation.

The best of the best and godliest of the godly was Hezekiah. "There was no king like him either before him or after him. Hezekiah remained true to the LORD" (2 Kings 18:5-6 NIRV). Even that was odd. (See number 155, "The Good King from Bad Stock.")

250

Borg Heaven

How big is heaven?

If Revelation's "new Jerusalem" is another name for heaven, and if we take literally the numbers that the writer, John, reports, heaven is a cube measuring 1400 miles (2200 km) in all directions (Revelation 21:16).

---

* 1 Samuel 13:14; 1 Kings 3:10,13; 15:11; 22:43; 2 Kings 18:5; 23:25

† 2 Chronicles 26:3; 27:2

In that case, a fleet of 150 million Borg spaceships could park efficiently in heaven. Borg ships from Star Trek films are cube-shaped. So is the new Jerusalem. It measures 2.7 billion cubic miles (4.3 billion cubic km). Reshaped into a ball, the new Jerusalem would be about half the size of the moon.

If everyone who ever lived—an estimated 106 billion souls—ended up in heaven, there would be about 40 souls per cubic mile (1.6 cubic km).

If all the souls had to cut their own grass, they'd be mowing the equivalent of about 16 NFL football fields—which might make heaven sound more like hell, especially to folks with grass allergies.

Many Bible experts say we're not supposed to take the numbers literally. Instead, they say the massive new Jerusalem is a symbol linked to the holiest spot on earth—a cube-shaped room in the back of the ancient Jewish temple. This temple was located, oddly enough, in what is now called the Old City of Jerusalem.

That holy room inside the temple measured 30 feet (9 m) in each direction. Called the Most Holy Place, this cube-shaped room housed the Jews' most sacred relic—the Ark of the Covenant, a gold-covered chest that held the Ten Commandments.

Only the high priest could go into this sacred room, and only once a year—on Yom Kippur, the Day of Atonement. That's when he sprinkled sacrificial blood on the Ark to atone for the sins of the entire Jewish nation.

The point of John's description of the new Jerusalem, many scholars say, is that heaven is unimaginably more holy than the holiest place on earth.

INDEX

Page numbers of primary entries are in bold.

More Great Books About the Bible
from Harvest House Publishers

A Quick Overview of the Bible
Douglas A. Jacoby

Dr. Jacoby bridges the gulf between the biblical world and the twenty-first century. He explains the big picture of the Bible, shows how the pieces fit together, provides the basic chronological outline of the Bible, and reveals the most important themes of the Old and New Testaments.

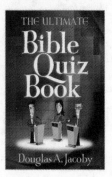

The Ultimate Bible Quiz Book
Douglas A. Jacoby

Who led a rebellion against Moses and Aaron?
Who was Jeremiah's secretary?
What was Peter's father's name?

These questions and countless more fill these entertaining one-page quizzes, with answers on the following page. Categories include important people in the Bible, books of the Bible, and many others.

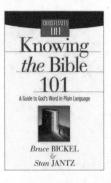

Knowing the Bible 101
Bruce Bickel and Stan Jantz

With extensive biblical knowledge and a contemporary perspective, Bruce Bickel and Stan Jantz provide a fun and user-friendly approach to understanding God's written message—its origin, themes, truth, and personal relevance.